PATCHWORK
plus!

Mary Jane Lamphier

Photographs: Bob Calmer
Cover Design: Jann Williams
Layout: Steve Pyle

Library of Congress
Catalog Card Number 82-060321

ISBN 0-87069-416-2
10 9 8 7 6 5 4 3 2 1

Published by

Wallace-Homestead Book Company
1912 Grand Avenue
Des Moines, Iowa 50305

Acknowledgments

My thanks to Betty Monkman, Registrar of the Office of the Curator in the White House; John Wickman, Director of the Dwight D. Eisenhower Library; Mary Matlow, patchwork demonstrator at the Seminole Okalee Village in Hollywood, Florida; Josephine Gaskill of Arlington, Iowa, collector of Bible Quilt blocks; Nancy Starr, Program Manager of the Smithsonian Institution, Washington, D.C.; and my friends and family for their encouragement and patience.

Contents

Patchwork, Past and Present

It was tough, that first winter in the New World. Not enough food. Colonists starved. Not enough heat. Colonists shivered as the warmth of wood fires escaped through the cracks in their hastily thrown up, makeshift shelters. They didn't even have piles of warm blankets to ease their lives. Death threatened every colonist, and death would have taken them . . . except for the women.

The women had needles and the women had scraps — tattered bits of worn-out clothing and other shreds of fabric. The women rose to the challenge of survival. Their answer to death that first winter in the New World?

Patchwork.

It was a homely solution, but the comforters they made with scraps and stuffed with scraps were survival gear. Some say that that survival gear later grew into a quilt "pattern" in its own right, called crazy patch.

Today it is difficult for us to realize that patchwork clothing and bedding was survival gear, but it is true.

During Colonial times, fabric was imported from England after England had imported it from India and other countries. After the seventeenth century, however, England began to manufacture textiles, and the settlers could purchase fabrics readily if they could afford them. Because of the high cost, the colonists began to grow flax to make their own linen and to raise sheep for the wool. Still, cloth continued in short supply because of the long, drawn-out process of converting flax and wool into usable fabric. Each raw material took a year or more of preparation before it was ready to weave.

According to history, the English did not encourage colonists to make fabric. They jealously hoarded patents for mechanical inventions contributing to the textile industry. This is understandable. After all, the production of yardgoods was a lucrative business. England wanted to monopolize the market. In fact, they wanted it so desperately that they imposed a cotton tax on the colonist.

By this time almost every home contained a spinning wheel and loom. Homespun materials were coarse and lacked color, but they served the purpose. It wasn't long before the colonists embarked on more self-sufficiency and began making dyes. They gathered bark from maple, oak, chestnut, and butternut trees to create dark colors. The berries of sumac

and other wild plants were the basis of brighter colors. Along with candlemaking, butchering, and barn raising, dyemaking was practiced by most settlers. Then and now, dyemaking resembled gourmet cooking. The chef hoarded the makings, adding a pinch of this and a dash of that, and stirred the steaming concoction in twenty-gallon kettles until the desired colors were produced.

The success of the dye often depended on the fabric and its preparation. The settlers discovered that dipping wool in an alum solution first, followed by a walnut shell solution, would produce a rich brown dye. Many experiments were made with dyes and fabrics. A combination of linen or cotton and wool was used in abundance. Its common name was linsey-woolsey. Successful recipes were passed from one family to another. Red and blue appear frequently in old patchwork quilts because the two colors were easily obtained from vegetable dyes.

From all this expertise, new specialists emerged called professional dyers. They served homemakers by dying their homespun fabric for them.

Home-grown labor was fully employed at an early age. Boys and girls helped with the carding, spinning, and weaving of wool and flax. If they were not busy with those chores, they were out scouring the countryside for raw materials to make dyes.

When fabric was ready to use, homemakers let nothing go to waste. Each pattern piece was carefully placed on the yardgoods to insure the least amount of waste. After a garment was cut out, the assorted leftover pieces were carefully stitched together by hand to form a large square to cover a bed. Often the front and back were nothing more than crazy patch pieced together from scraps. With the absence of traditional batting (cotton or wool), early quilters substituted dry grass, feathers, cornhusks, or rags. Needless to say, the quilts of that era did not resemble what we recognize as quilts today. Rather than a minute ten stitches to the inch, the layers were fastened together with long running stitches and heavy cord.

Many hours were spent producing, repairing, and cleaning quilts. Quilt care usually consisted of removing the batting (such as it was), washing the outside cover, and putting the layers back together.

It wasn't until Eli Whitney invented the cotton gin in 1793 that the industrial revolution was here for good. With new cotton mills following, an abundance of cotton material was now available to the American housewife. By 1850 the country was flooded with soft calicos and cottons.

Then something strange began to happen. Patchwork quilts were no longer merely necessities in lonely rural cabins. Unpredictably, patchwork was becoming a quality craft . . . a means of decorating the home, of adding embellishment and charm. The crazy patch was appearing in satins and velvets, outlined in lovely gold floss with fancy stitches.

Imaginative people created patchwork patterns from triangles, squares, and rectangles. They sat down and planned a quilt's design, color, and fabric with the numerous choices now available to them. The day of choice was a spur to creativity in patchwork.

New patterns that were named for familiar surroundings appeared. Some of the first were log cabin, goose tracks, bear claw, and pine tree. Blocks were named after a trade like dusty miller, and more than a few were taken from the Bible. Political quilt blocks were also popular. They were named after the kings and queens of the Old World and, as our country grew and became independent, after the presidents of the republic. Quilters also tacked the first names of the presidents' wives to patterns or made use of other political subjects. Clay's Choice, Martha Washington's Star, Lincoln's Platform, Square Deal, and Roosevelt Rose are examples. State quilts were another popular group of patchwork patterns. During the Civil War the eagle made its debut on printed fabric. The national emblem soon appeared everywhere, perched sedately in a sky of patchwork and applique.

One of the most famous eagle quilts was made in 1846. It is the Smithsonian Institution's Quilt, which is also called the President's Quilt.

Quite obviously, much of America's history is recorded in quilts. As settlers moved deeper into the unexplored West, patterns depicting the way of life went with them.

Frontier traditions formed around patchwork and quilting. One early household rule was that each young woman must piece thirteen quilts before she married. And if she didn't? Look out lady! If, by chance, she had not a single quilt finished by the age of twenty-one, the maiden was destined to be an old maid. But on the other hand, it was considered unwise to hurry and finish a bridal quilt before engagement.

That might bring bad luck to a later marriage—or perhaps even stop one.

Many other superstitions involved the quilt. Wandering Foot was an undesirable quilt for a potential bride. No mother would encourage her daughter to use that pattern for fear that her man, when he appeared, would turn out to be a card shark or some other social misfit. Pattern choice was of the utmost importance. A young woman was encouraged not to stray from the reliable path of the tried-and-true. The Double Wedding Ring pattern was a sure winner.

Bride's quilts were often assembled at quilting bees, occasions for friends and neighbors to congregate and help sew. Mothers and daughters attended, loaded with food, patterns, and pincushions. A quilting bee was a social event, to say the least. Children played under the quilt frame, and men conversed by the fire. After the quilt was completed, dancing and singing was not uncommon. Usually a delightful lunch was served—homemade biscuits and jelly, accompanied with a jug of apple cider.

Elaborate friendship quilts were made at quilting parties, too. Each guest arrived with a finished block. The blocks were sewn together, and in one afternoon, the backing, batting, and top were stitched. Women made the rounds from house to house until each owned a friendship quilt, a highly treasured heirloom. These quilts were generally used for display only, resting on a spare bed or hanging on a wall.

Album and presentation quilts were assembled in the same way. A group of people, admiring the clergyman and his wife, might decide to give them a gift—a presentation quilt. These were examples of excellent workmanship. No one dare to get lazy! Instead, quilters vied with one another to make the most beautiful block. In return, the recipient of the elaborate gift did not toss this labor of love on the everyday bed. It was a prized possession to be saved for special occasions.

Another colorful quilt is the sampler, which is made up of a collection of patterns with each block being different. I find them often today at quilt shows. Most adhere to a specific color scheme, such a the earth-tone color scheme of the Bible Block Quilt in this book.

I have come to the conclusion that in the past, whatever the occasion was, there was a quilt for it. Memory quilts were the most morbid. They were made from the clothes of the deceased. New babies were presented with small and delicate quilts, as they are today. Young people were offered cot quilts and, when they graduated to a larger bed, they were again presented with a quilt of their own. At the age of twenty-one, boys were given freedom quilts.

There were summer quilts and winter quilts, differing in color and weight, with thin pastel fabrics used for warm weather and heavy dark ones for cold. Gay and gaudy quilts, lovely artistic patchwork quilts—it's no surprise that quilt making became a competitive game.

In 1808 the first county fair turned competitive quilt making public. No longer did only family and friends race to outdo one another for the fun of it. Avid quilters now had the opportunity to pool new patterns, collect beautiful fabrics, gather lovely embroidery flosses, and display before the eyes of all their best possible workmanship. They had a driving passion to make a masterpiece worthy of ribbons and prizes, not to mention gaining coveted fame.

As expected, the challenge was met with enthusiasm, and the public benefited from the ardor of craftspeople. During the War of 1812, contests were promoted to help keep citizens busy and to aid in soothing the unrest of the era. Yankee peddlers took to the road and sold, traded, and bartered. They offered bolts of assorted calicoes, battings, flosses, muslins, and patterns in exchange for produce and pelts.

Nimble fingers continued to work from dawn to dusk and on in lamplight, slowly finishing patchwork quilts as gifts for birthdays, weddings, and, now, for competition in the fairs.

Meanwhile Howe and Singer were putting their heads together, and by 1860 they consolidated ideas, and the sewing machine became common in households. Women set aside their thimbles and pulled up a chair to the manual machines. They could make patchwork quilt tops in less than half the previous time. The quilt population exploded. Competition intensified at the county fairs, and everyone was enjoying the game.

Industry took advantage of the sewing machine and ready-to-wear clothing companies were established. These expanded to blanket production, and by the early 1900s, there was a noticeable decline in hand-made patchwork quilts. Quilting may have been popular in individual parlors, but it was not a public rage during the first half of the twentieth century. But

in 1960 a comeback of interest in piecework was apparent. In both 1961 and 1962, proficient quilters presented the president of the United States with a quilt. Like the late nineteenth and early twentieth century presentation quilts, those in the 1960s were given with love and respect. These were personal gifts and did not remain at the White House. As a president finished his term, he took the quilt with him.

Patchwork and quilting gained popularity through books, magazines and contests. Contests were no longer confined to local communities. The world seemed to be getting smaller as national contests and world fairs promoted quilt exhibits.

In addition, collections of quilts flourished throughout the country. People were beginning to realize the value of patchwork as art. The Dwight D. Eisenhower Boyhood Home Collection is exhibited at the Eisenhower Library in Abilene, Kansas. The collection consits of thirteen quilts made by Ida Stover Eisenhower, mother of the thirty-fourth president of the United States. Some of the quilts are Grandmother's Flower Garden, made of cotton; Turkey Tracks, cotton; Sawtooth, wool and cotton; crazy patch, velvet, wool, cotton, and silk; and a beautiful crazy patch in lavish velvets.

Perhaps the quilt show of all quilt shows in the United States is in the Smithsonian Institution. The quilt collection at the National Museum of American History, Smithsonian Institution, is one of the finest collections in the U.S. It includes approximately 300 quilts that represent a wide variety of types, materials, and techniques used in America from the eighteenth century through the early twentieth century. In 1982 the Smithsonian also aided quilters by offering a week-long seminar in its Selected Studies Program called, "Quilting: Traditional to Modern, the Secrets of Success."

Our nation's capitol has shown other interest in patchwork. At Christmastime in 1974, the imaginative first lady Betty Ford and her daughter Susan found their sewing baskets and sorted out laces and silks and ribbons. The two designed an ornament for the White House Christmas tree. Mrs. Ford embroidered "Betty Ford for 74" on hers and hung it on the nineteen-foot fir in the middle of the Blue Room, where it mingled with 550 other patchwork balls and Christmas lanterns. The assortment of patchwork trimmings was contributed by senior citizens and craftspeople in states throughout the nation. The White House also had patchwork bows and wreaths to welcome guests. In the entrance foyer, visitors were greeted by eleven angels whose delicate robes were lined with patchwork. The Red Room sported a charming velvet table cover in old-fashioned crazy patch, done in warm and brilliant colors. Traditional patchwork was the theme of the season.

In 1976, the year of America's Bicentennial, patchwork was again in the limelight. Another historical quilt pattern was born, the Bicentennial Star. It grew from the American Revolution Bicentennial Administration symbol, and was, of course, made with patriotic red, white, and blue.

Quilts emerged from coast to coast in honor of the celebration. Ethel Zwanziger of Strawberry Point, Iowa, designed a quilt of twenty flags that had at one time or another flown over the White House. She started with the flag of our nation when under English rule, added one with a black stripe that was flown at the time of Lincoln's assassination, and many more, most of which had flown over the White House. The quilt now hangs in the Strawberry Point Museum, an example of the enthusiasm demonstrated by quilters that year.

Presidents' quilts are also returning. Gunilla Caufield of Newburyport, Massachusetts, presented President Carter with a quilt in commemoration of the return of the American hostages from Iran in January, 1981. The center of the quilt is a patchwork design, the Eastern Star pattern. On each star a hostage's name is embroidered. The quilting is the Liberty Bell and the Statue of Liberty. Around the border is an unforgettable yellow ribbon, recalling a tradition dating back to Civil War days when people with loved ones in the service hung a yellow ribbon and prayed for their safe return.

It is evident that an undaunted interest in patchwork quilts and small items continues to flourish.

General Information

Quilt pieces. Before you start any project, wash and dry the fabric. This will shrink the material, remove any finish applied to the fiber, and determine color fastness. Next, trim all selvages. They are more tightly woven and often are printed or colored differently by the fabric designer or manufacturer. Press the yardgoods. Cut patterns with the grain of the fabric. In polyester and cotton blends, there is often a directional sheen. Cut all quilt pieces in the same direction to avoid distressing confusion. Except where noted, all fabrics listed in this book are 45" wide.

Needles and threads. A glaze is applied to quilting, button, carpet, and polyspun threads to provide a hard surface and make it easier to pull them through fabric. When selecting thread for a quilt, quilting thread is not the only alternative. Some quilters like synthetic thread, which is a three-strand thread. Each strand is continuous filament polyester wrapped in cotton. I am, however, a firm believer in using only quilting thread for the actual quilting. When quilting, use a small needle that will not leave large, unsightly needle tracks. Cut thread from the spool. Do not bite it! The threading of a needle can be tedious when using frayed ends, and we are striving for organization and smooth operation from start to finish.

Patterns. The patterns in this book are actual-sized templates. Cut out the pattern, lay it on the *wrong side* of the fabric, and draw around it. The pencil or chalk mark is the seamline. Add the seam allowance as you cut the fabric. Quilt pieces are given ¼" seams, as a rule.

Press the seams with your thumbnail as you sew. Trim extra fabric from corners and curves. Construct one block at a time, and press when it is completed. After all the blocks are finished, either pin or paste them together in proper sequence. Sew them together and press seams. Check the surface of the quilt top. Does it lie flat? If there are problem areas, now is the time to fix them.

If there is trouble, it could be in the assembly of a chosen pattern. Hexagonal and curved patterns are done entirely by hand. It is difficult to match them perfectly on a sewing machine. Some patterns require full concentration, and it is helpful to keep the diagram before you.

The ability to divide the more difficult patterns, those with two dozen pieces or more, is soon learned. Divide the block into separate sections, completing each section and joining them by rows. After laying a grid over the pattern, the most complex designs become understandable.

Borders. The frame of the quilt may be one of three general styles; patchwork, applique, or quilting. Those in this book are all quilted, but with noticeable differences.

Linings. My choice of lining is a bed sheet. They come in a variety of sizes and thread counts. Avoid sheets with a thread count of 180. These are too closely woven to push a needle through easily. The sheet I used to line the Wildflower Quilt is light blue with a thread count of 130. It is an attractive polyester and cotton percale. The Bible Quilt is lined with the same sheet in brown. In fact, I also use sheets to line wall hangings, purses, and pillows. Some people, however, prefer fabric exactly like the quilt top. Whatever is used, lining should be seamed twice. Avoid making a single seam down the center, and the reverse side will be more attractive.

Interlinings. The interlining may be cotton, wool, a flannel sheet, another old quilt (which I do not recommend), a sheet, or the most popular modern product, polyester batting. Polyester battings come in a variety of sizes and weights. If you want a thicker, loftier quilt, buy heavyweight batting. Polyester batting is also available by the yard. Some yardages must be overlapped to cover a quilt, which can cause bulky ridges. Another problem with poor grade products is pilling through the needle holes in the quilt fabric. I have not had this trouble, but I always use quality filling with a glazene finish for easier handling. Some batting is bonded for easier handling, but beware. Sometimes these products are stiff as a board, very thin, or tacky.

Technique. When spreading batting be careful not to pull it too strongly and create thin spots. Gently lift and spread the fibers on the lining.

When sewing the lining and top to the quilt frame, do so in the seam allowance along the edge. Don't pull thread too tight or you may tear the fabric.

Applique is used often in this book, and here are a few tips to save time and patience. Use freezer paper. It is a quilter's blessing. It comes in two varieties, and I recommend the plastic coated type. I find polyethylene coated 17½" × 33⅓" rolls in my local food store. The paper is durable and sufficiently transparent for easy tracing. To make the pattern the same as you view it, place the dull side of the paper on the pattern and trace on the shiny side. Cut out the paper template. Press the template, shiny side to the fabric, and cut fabric ¼″ beyond the template for the seam allowance. Use a dry iron on cotton setting. Press the seam allowance toward the center of the motif. Clip the seam allowance *only* if you cannot get it to lie flat on small, sharp curves. I peel the freezer paper from the wrong side of the fabric and reverse it if the pattern is symmetrical (the same on both sides of a dividing line). If it is not symmetrical, draw another template, placing the shiny side down on the pattern and drawing on the dull side. Place the new template (or the first one—they are reusable) on the wrong side of the fabric. The shiny side is now up. Press the seam allowance over the edge of the freezer paper. The applique seam allowance is fused in place and will have a sharper crease. Leave it fused until you are ready to applique.

Except where noted, all seam allowances in this book are ¼″.

1. Cross-stitch

Make a row of evenly spaced slanted stitches of equal length. Work over them in the opposite direction with the same length of evenly spaced, slanted stitches.

2. Backstitch

Take short stitches, inserting the needle at the end of the previous stitch. Bring needle out a stitch ahead of the free thread. Stitches will resemble those made by a sewing machine.

3. Straight stitch

Straight stitches may go in any direction and be of any length. In this example, ⅜″ stitches radiate around a ½″ circle. Insert needle in fabric and bring it out at the "center" to begin another stitch.

4. Lazy daisy stitch

Bring thread out on the pattern line, inserting needle next to where the thread emerged. Keep thread under the needle to form a loop. Insert needle again a little below the loop and bring it out once more wherever the next stitch is desired.

5. Chainstitch

This stitch is used in this book to outline, because it is easy to make curved lines with it. Bring thread out on the pattern line. Insert needle next to where the thread emerged. Keep the thread under the needle and form a loop. Insert needle where the needle emerged.

6. Herringbone stitch

This is the open herringbone stitch. Work from left to right along two imaginary parallel lines. Mark the lines lightly if you cannot follow the weave of the fabric. Bring the needle out on the lower left. Take a short backstitch on the upper line a little to the right. Keep thread under the needle. Take a backstitch on the lower line a little to the right. Keep spaces between stitches even.

7. Satin stitch

The satin stitch should completely cover the underlying fabric. Stitch in any direction, using short stitches and making an even edge. For a padded effect go around the pattern line with straight stitches before covering all with smooth satin stitches.

8. Quilting (running) stitch

Stitches may be long or short, but should be evenly spaced as you run the needle in and out of the fabric. This stitch is used for quilting (small stitches) and sewing by hand.

9. French knot

Bring thread up through fabric, wind thread around the needle with your left hand two, three, or more times (the more windings, the larger the knot). Insert the needle close to where it emerged and pull to the wrong side, forming a knot.

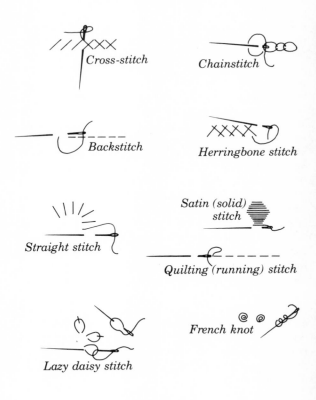

Cross-stitch

Chainstitch

Backstitch

Herringbone stitch

Straight stitch

Satin (solid) stitch

Quilting (running) stitch

Lazy daisy stitch

French knot

Embroidery Guide

Quilts

Field of Wildflowers Quilt

Every quilt has a story. The Field of Wildflowers Quilt was created because of my love of nature. I am fortunate to live near one of Iowa's most striking areas for varied flora. In the spring, Brush Creek Canyon State Preserve in Fayette County comes to life with a large variety of wildflowers, and most of the flowers on the quilt were found there.

I have had much help and many suggestions from loved ones, but often the question has arisen, what is a wildflower and what is a weed? Although many object to the thistle, in my eyes it is a beautiful flower. The milkweed is another questionable plant, but it is fascinating. Its flower is lavender, but I am more entranced with the pod and seeds later in the season. Thus it appears in the quilt in this form.

The wild rose appears in the quilt three times to show its variation of color from delicate pink to deep red.

The quilt is appliqued. Embroidery is used to bring out details. But please don't search for every sepal, seed, or exact color. This is a symbolic representation of the beauty I find around me.

Wild rose	Milk-weed	Columbine	Mayapple	Wild rose
Thistle	Marsh marigold	Wild ginger	Violet (yellow)	Skunk cabbage
Black-eyed Susan	Dandelion	Showy orchis	Red clover	Oxeye daisy
Dutchman's breeches	Wild bergamot	Wild strawberry	Bloodroot	Trout lily (yellow)
Trillium (purple)	Wood sorrel	Rose #2	Money wort	Trillium (white)
Lady's slipper (yellow)	Aster (purple)	Jack-in-the-pulpit	Cone-flower (purple)	Lady's slipper (pink)

Placement of Wildflower Quilt blocks

Materials:

Fabric	Yardage
Blue	8
Gold	1
Dark green	⅓
Medium green	⅓
Light green	⅓
Grey green	⅛
Dark rose	¼
Pale pink	¼
Red (coordinate with pink)	¼
Wine red	⅛
Brown	¼
Purple	¼
White	¼
Bright yellow	¼
Sewing thread to match fabrics	1 spool each
Gold, purple, light green, dark green, deep pinkish lavender, medium green, wine red (op.) embroidery floss	1 skein each
Blue quilting thread	1 250-yard spool
Batting	81″ × 96″
Sheet	81″ × 96″

Method:

Step 1. Cut border strips from blue fabric: 2 end borders 10″ × 62″; 2 side borders 10″ × 92″. Don't piece unless it is necessary to match sheen. These figures are generous. Trim after border is attached to quilt top.

Step 2. Cut thirty 13″ blocks from blue fabric. *This will allow ½″ seam allowance. Finished blocks in quilt will be 12″ square.*

Step 3. Cut sixteen 1½″ × 45″ strips from gold fabric. This is the inside border and tape for the outer edge. Set all pieces aside.

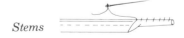

Stems

Step 4. Make flower stems by cutting strips on the bias 1½″ wide from the green fabric required in a specific block. Cutting on the bias eases making the curved lines of the stems. Fold edges of strips together and press. The bias tape will be ¾″ wide. Pin tape to designated area on block. Stitch through center (dash line). Trim seam allowance. Fold pressed edge over and applique along crease.

You can vary stem width by adjusting the seam allowance width on the stem. Most stem ends are covered with flowers or leaves, but in some instances fold ends to the inside before stitching to the blue block.

Step 5. Make flower blocks as follows, adding seam allowance to all patterns. Applique and press as you go.

Wild Rose. Cut a 3″ bias strip for a ⅛″ stem. Cut 4 medium green leaves (a), 1 deep pink rose (c), and 1 yellow center (b). In upper center of the block, sew leaf stem first, then pink rose, and last, yellow center. Chainstitch gold spots on center of the flower. To separate rose petals, chainstitch on dotted lines with pink floss. Repeat on separate block using pale pink fabric.

| Wild rose | Milkweed |

Milkweed. Make a dark green stem, 6″ × ¼″. Applique stem to center of block. Cut 2 leaves of dark green (right, a, and left, b) and 1 gray green pod (c). Applique both to stem. Embroider light green inverted V's on pod using straight stitches. This gives texture.

Columbine. Make an 8″ × ¼″ stem from brown fabric. Applique stem to block. Cut one red flower and applique to stem. Chainstitch on dotted lines with red floss to separate petals. Chainstitch gold pistils.

| Columbine | Mayapple |

Mayapple. Make a 6″ × ¼″ green stem. Cut 1 medium green leaf (a) and 1 white flower (b). Applique stem, leaf, then flower to block. Embroider center of flower with gold satin stitch and chainstitch veins of leaf on dotted lines with medium green floss.

Thistle. The stem of this flower is made from pattern (d). Cut 1 stem, 2 leaves (c), and 1 lower bulb (b) from gray green. Cut 1 purple bloom (a). Applique leaves, covering ends with stem. Applique bulb to stem, leaving top edge unturned and flat. Applique purple bloom over it. Embroider vertical dashes (straight stitches) throughout the bloom with lavender floss. Some of these should extend over purple fabric to indicate the thorns of the thistle. With green floss, embroider inverted Vs on bulb using straight stitches.

| Thistle | Marsh marigold |

Marsh marigold. Another name for this wildflower is cowslip. Make a medium green 7″ × ¼″ stem. Make another stem 2″ long and a third, 1½″. Applique large medium green leaf (b) to center of block. Applique main stem to center of leaf. Add short stems to main stem. Cover intersection with a small circle of medium green fabric. Hide stem tops with 3 gold marigolds (a). Chainstitch centers with gold floss. Add small medium green leaf (c) to stem bottom.

Wild ginger. Make 2 dark green stems, one 5″ × ¼″ and the other 5½″ × ¼″. Applique stems to center of block. Cut 2 large, dark green leaves (a) and applique to tops of stems. Chainstitch light green veins in leaves. Cut 6 wine red petals (b) and applique 3 together to form a flower. Make 1 small medium green leaf (c) for bottom of stem.

| Wild ginger | Violet (yellow) |

Violet (yellow). Violets, or Johnny-jumpups, are typically found in shades of blue and purple. Yellow violets are scarce. Make three 6″ stems and two 3″ stems in medium green and very narrow. Applique to center of block, starting at a common point on the lower end. Cover lower ends with one medium green leaf (a). Applique another medium green leaf (a) to right-hand stem. Make 4 yellow violets (b) and applique to remaining stems. Embroider straight stitch white lines from flower center and gold French knots in center.

Skunk cabbage. The skunk cabbage is one plant I cannot find in my area. Its true color is a mottled brown, but artists often picture it deep purple. Cut 1 purple center piece (a) and 2 dark green outer leaves (right, c, and left b). Applique purple first, leaving lower edge unturned. Cover lower edge with green. Chainstitch purple line on center piece.

Skunk cabbage   Black-eyed Susan/ Oxeye daisy

Black-eyed Susan. Make 4″ × ¼″ stem of dark green. Applique stem to block. Cut 1 gold flower (a) and 1 brown center (b). Applique and chainstitch with gold to outline petals.

Oxeye daisy. Use black-eyed Susan pattern, making flower white and center yellow.

Dandelion. To make the "lion of the lawn," you will need 1 light green stem 6″ × ¼″ and one 5″ × ¼″. Applique stems first. Add 2 dark green leaves (1a and 1d) and dark green (c) and yellow (b) flowers. Overlap c on b. Embroider yellow straight stitch lines to edge flower and define veinlines in leaves with chain stitches.

Dandelion   Showy orchis

Showy orchis. The purple showy orchis is a rare wildflower in my favorite woods. Its habitat is precariously close to a well trodden footpath. You will need a 6″ × ¼″ dark green stem. Applique stem first. Cover lower edge with 2 dark green leaves (a and b). Cut 6 purple, tear-shaped petals (3c and 3d) and 3 white ones (c). Each of the 3 flowers has 2 purple tears at top (1c and 1d) and 1 white tear at

bottom center. Applique white tear first. Layer purple tears on top right and left of white tear. Chainstitch dark green veins in leaves.

Red clover. No wonder bees love the clover. What fragrance! Make 2 medium green stems, one 6″ × ¼″ and the other 5″ × ¼″. Applique them first. Cut 2 purple clover heads (a) and applique. Add medium green leaves (2b and 2c) last. Chainstitch with lavender to completely cover clover head, extending stitches over edge of purple fabric to produce a soft clover look.

 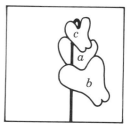

Red clover   Dutchman's-breeches

Dutchman's-breeches. It sets my heart to tickin', as Frost said, when I see the tiny white bloomers dancing in the breeze. You will need a 10″ × ¼″ light green stem, but don't sew it on yet. Cut center breeches (a) and applique to block. Applique stem over breeches. Cut top breeches (c) and applique. Add bottom breeches (b) and shade lower areas of top and bottom breeches with gold chainstitches.

Wild bergamot. Some call this wildflower bee balm or horsemint. Both leaves and stem have a minty aroma, and people do use them for tea. The flower ranges in color from pink to lavender to purple. To solve the color problem, I combined purple fabric with lavender embroidery. Make a gray green stem 6″ × ¼″. Applique stem first. Add 2 leaves (1d and 1e) to the bottom. Cut 1 purple flower (a) and applique to stem. Applique 2 gray green sepals (1b and 1c) to lower edge of flower. Straightstitch flower (a) to give it a shaggy look.

Wild bergamot   Wild strawberry

Wild strawberry. I call this Mary Ellen's block. My daughter-in-law was looking at the flowers and said, "You need a wild strawberry." She helped me design the plant, and she insisted it must have ripe red berries. Start by making 2 medium green 1″ × ¼″ stems for the leaves. Place stems first. Add center leaf (c), medium green, followed by 2 leaves (c) on the side. Make 3 red berries (a) and 3 white flowers (b). Applique into place. Chainstitch gold centers on flowers. Give berries gold French knot seeds. Chainstitch green veins on leaves and green Calyx on berries.

Bloodroot. Bloodroot is an early spring flower. The leaf is light green underneath but darker on top, and the flowers are white. Make a 6″ × ¼″ stem. Add white flower (a) to top and medium green leaf (b) on the bottom. Chainstitch outlines of petals with white floss.

Bloodroot *Trout lily (yellow)*

Trout lily (yellow). Make a 6″ × ¼″ stem and 2 dark green leaves (b). The flower (a) is bright yellow. Place pattern on fold of fabric and cut 1. Chainstitch outline of petals and apply gold French knots to center pistils.

Trillium (purple). Make a 7″ × ¼″ stem of medium green. Cut purple flower (a) and 3 medium green leaves (1b, 1c, and 1d). Applique stem, pin flower in place so it overlaps on leaves, and position leaves. Applique leaves, then flower. Add an embroidered gold center to flower, using lazy daisy stitches. Make white trillium in the same manner.

Trillium *Wood sorrel*

Wood sorrel. Make 2 light green leaves (each leaf is 3 b pieces) and 2 white flowers (a). Add pink chainstitches on dotted lines to define petals and make 4 or 5 gold French knots in the center.

Rose #2. This is one of the brightly colored roses found along our roadsides. It produces the rose hips eaten by birds. Make an 8″ × ¼″ stem and a 4″ × ¼″ stem. The third stem measures 1″ × ⅛″. Use dark green. Cut 11 leaves (c). Applique red rose (a) next. Give rose a yellow fabric center. Add red hip (b) last.

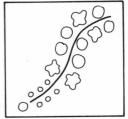

Rose #2 *Moneywort*

Moneywort. When Aunt Elsie saw the moneywort, she grabbed her husband's arm and ushered him to the sewing room. "Look what she has in her wildflower quilt. That creeping Charlie we've been fighting for years!" Then they both laughed. Make a 13″ stem of dark green. Taper end to ⅛″. Cut 6 dark green larger, coin-shaped leaves (b), 7 dark green medium-sized leaves (c), and 4 bright yellow flowers (a). Applique stem, then add leaves and flowers. Chainstitch dark green veins in leaves.

Lady's slipper (yellow). I found a cluster of seven of these lovely lady's slippers. Make a light green stem 8″ × ¼″. Applique to block. Cut 2 leaves (1b and 1c) and 2 sepals (1d and 1e). Applique. Add yellow slipper (a). Chainstitch small round section on the top of slipper with gold floss. Make pink lady's slipper in same manner, using deep pink fabric.

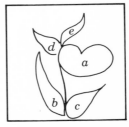

Lady's slipper (yellow) *Aster (purple)*

Aster (purple). Make an 8″ × ¼″ main stem. Pin in place. Cut four 2½″ stems of dark green and sew in place with their lower ends under main stem. Add 5 purple flowers (b) and 3 dark green leaves (a). Chainstitch gold centers in asters.

Jack-in-the-pulpit. Make a 7″ × ½″ stem of medium green and a second stem 3½″ × ½″. Applique 7″

14

stem. Cover lower end with medium green main flower (a). Add medium green underleaf (b) to top of stem. Layer medium green second leaf (c). Applique shorter stem and add a leaf (d) to top. Pistil (e) may be pieced or embroidered with satin stitches. Use either medium green or wine red floss, depending on the age of your Jack-in-the-pulpit.

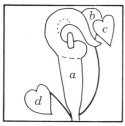 

Jack-in-the-pulpit   Coneflower (purple)

Coneflower (purple). Cut 2 stems, one $8'' \times \frac{1}{4}''$ and the other $4'' \times \frac{1}{4}''$. These are appliqued first. Add a dark green leaf (c), and a purple head (a) to top left stem. Add full bloom (b) to right stem. Applique second leaf (c) to bottom of right stem. Chainstitch petal outline with purple floss. Make small lazy daisy stitches on flower heads. Chainstitch dark green vein lines on leaves.

Step 6. Set blocks together easily, using the placement chart. Pin first row together. Press seams after first five blocks are sewn in place. When six rows are finished, sew them together to form a $60'' \times 72''$ rectangle. *Remember the seam allowance for the blocks and border is $\frac{1}{2}''$.*

The quilt's design has been balanced by placing small flowers in the center and large flowers around the edge, with a rose in each upper corner and a lady's slipper in each lower corner. The colors are also evenly distributed. We would not want a large splash of bright yellow in one area and white in another. Because of the small number of red flowers, they are placed down the center.

Step 7. Sew gold strips together, end to end. Press in half to make a double thickness. This is a $\frac{3}{4}''$ border. Baste strip to top and bottom of field of flowers. Use a $\frac{1}{4}''$ seam allowance to create a border $\frac{1}{2}''$ wide. Pin blue border to gold, right sides

together. This would be the $10'' \times 62''$ pieces. Sew borders to top and bottom. Baste gold strip to sides. Cut gold fabric $\frac{1}{2}''$ longer than the meeting point of the gold border on top and bottom. Turn in edges and baste in place. Sew on $10'' \times 92''$ border. Press seams, placing folded edge of gold border facing outside edge of finished quilt.

Step 8. Set up quilting frames and place sheet, batting, and quilt top together in the traditional sandwich layout. Start at one end and work to the other. I started with the last row on the quilt so I could work with flowers in a normal position. Quilt around each appliqued flower, $\frac{1}{8}''$ from the edge of the design. Quilt around each flower two more times at $\frac{1}{2}''$ intervals.

The four-leaf clover pattern is used in areas where quilting is distant. Pin pattern down, trace around it with a dressmaker's chalk, and quilt on the chalkline. You will find the need for the clover at most block intersections.

Step 9. Quilting the border will go rapidly. It is a framework of straight lines. Start by quilting $\frac{1}{8}''$ from edge of gold border, or $\frac{5}{8}''$ from the field of flowers and border seam. Take a chalk pencil and a ruler and mark $2''$ from the last quilted line. Quilt around the border three times at $2''$ intervals.

When quilting is finished, remove quilt from frame and trim extra batting and lining to make a neat, even edge. Finish edges with gold strips. Sew strips, one thickness, right sides of fabric together, $\frac{1}{4}''$ seam to the top and bottom. Fold in $\frac{1}{4}''$ at each end on last two side strips. Turn under a $\frac{1}{4}''$ hem on back and blindstitch to lining of quilt.

Bible Blocks Quilt

The Bible Blocks Quilt can be classified as either a theme quilt or a sampler quilt. Most of the Bible blocks are traditional patterns passed down from generation to generation. In this collection, some are patchwork squares and triangles, others are applique, and a few, like Forbidden Fruit and Tree of Life, are a combination.

Directions are for a double-bed sized quilt measuring 78″×97″. A completed block is 14″ square plus seam allowance. When lattice and blocks are joined together, blocks will measure 14″ exactly.

One of your first decisions is color scheme. Keep in mind that this is an excellent pattern for sewing scraps. Josephine Gaskill of Arlington, Iowa, made a Bible Blocks Quilt from odds and ends left over from her sewing projects, and it is beautiful. Since my ragbag was depleted long ago, I decided to use earth tones, with a soft brown for lattice and border. I found a sheet in nearly the same brown for lining. The earth tones blend together, and you may mix and match to please yourself. However, directions are given for the colors I used. Of course each quilt will be unique because the prints and tones will vary. One bit of advice—shop with samples in hand to achieve a good color combination.

Materials:

Fabric	Yardage
Brown broadcloth for lattice	5
Brown double-bed sized sheet	1
Solids:	
White	1
Gold	1
Light green	½
Orange	½
Brown (same as lattice fabric)	½
Yellow	½
Prints:	
#1 Orange print (light orange, large design)	½
#2 Orange print (dark orange, small design)	½
#1 Brown (with small white and green figures)	½
#2 Brown (with small white flowers)	½
#3 Brown (with small white and yellow figures)	½
Brown dotted	½
Light brown print	½
Light green print	½
Medium green print	½
Gold print	½
Yellow print	½
Embroidery floss:	

Gold	5 skeins
White	1 skein
Quilting thread:	
Brown, gold, orange, white	1 spool each
Polyester batting	81″×96″

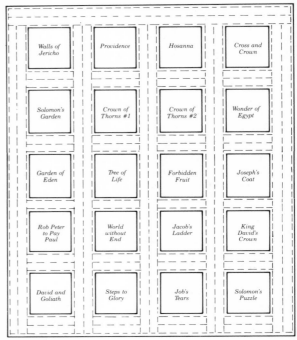

Placement of Bible Quilt blocks
(with quilting lines of border and lattice)

Method:

Step 1. Cut one block pattern at a time. Make template from freezer paper, and press to *wrong side* of fabric. Cut fabric ¼″ from edge of template for seam allowance. Leave fabric and template fused until after block is stitched. (Freezer paper makes a stable seam guide.) Peel off paper and press block.

Stitch small pieces like those in the Forbidden Fruit block by hand to avoid your machine's feed dog devouring the fabric.

Check accuracy of each block. It should be exactly 14″, plus seam allowance. If your block is not true, you may alter it before you join the lattice. If it is completely out of kilter (this should never happen if you follow directions), remake block.

Walls of Jericho (Josh. 6:20). Cut 4 white (a), 4 #1 orange print (b), 4 #1 brown print (c), 1 gold (d), 4

Field of Wildflowers Quilt

Bible Blocks Quilt

The Old Swimming Hole Quilt

Handkerchief Print Pillow

Seminole Patchwork: Pillow, Apron, Shopping Bag, Glasses Case

Checkerboard Pillow

21

Spotty Dog, Digger

Bunny in the Berry Patch

Saturday Night

#2 brown print (e). Sew a, b, and c together to make corner squares. Make center strip (e, d, and e). Connect two squares in top row with e. Do the same for the bottom row. Sew the three rows together.

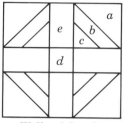

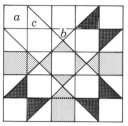

Walls of Jericho   Providence

Providence (The guiding power of the universe). Cut 8 #3 brown print (c), 8 gold (c), 9 gold (a), 4 gold print (a), 8 gold print (b), and 8 gold (b).

Hosanna (John 12:12). Cut 1 yellow (a), 2 yellow print (b), 2 yellow (c), 2 gold (d), 2 yellow (e), 2 gold print (f), and 2 yellow (g). Fold the material right sides of fabric together to make opposing patterns. Sew b and c together, d and e together, and f and g together. Press and sew c to d and e to f. Make the opposing unit and sew the two sections together, matching b, d, and f. Sew the square (a) in the corner last.

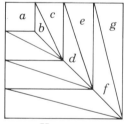

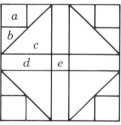

Hosanna   Cross and Crown

Cross and Crown (Matt. 27:32-40). Cut 4 white (a), 8 white (b), 8 #3 brown print (b), 4 orange (c), 4 #1 orange print (d), and 1 #3 brown print (e). Sew the corner pieces (b) together. Add (a) piece, press, and attach (c) piece. Make four identical sections. Connect two sections with a (d) piece. Make the center strip by sewing (d), (e), and (d) together. Sew the three sections together.

Solomon's Garden (Song of Sol. 4:12-16). Cut 1 white hexagon (a), 1 gold star (b), and 1 small orange hexagon (c). Applique white hexagon to a 15″ square gold piece. Applique gold star to hexagon. Applique orange hexagon to star. Embroider daisies on star points, using chainstitches. Outline

orange hexagon and divide star points with white chain stitches.

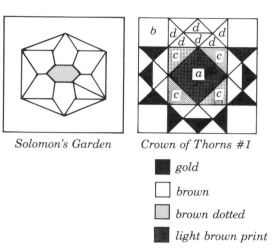

Solomon's Garden   Crown of Thorns #1

▪ gold
☐ brown
▨ brown dotted
▪ light brown print

Crown of Thorns #1 (Mark 15:17). Cut 1 light brown print (a), 4 brown (b), 12 brown dotted (d), 12 gold (d), 8 brown (d), and 4 brown dotted (c). Start with the center square (a) and add 4 corners (c). Make four side pieces, each with 3 brown dotted (d) and 1 gold (d). Sew side pieces to center square. Make the outer corner (b) and 4 (d). Sew this to center as shown.

Crown of Thorns #2 (John 19:2). Cut 5 light green (a), 16 light green (b), 12 #1 brown print (b), 4 #2 orange print (b), 4 #2 orange print (a). Sew together row by row according to diagram.

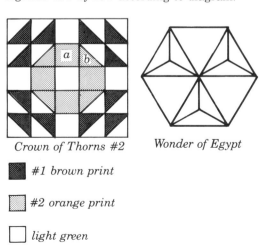

Crown of Thorns #2   Wonder of Egypt

▪ #1 brown print
▨ #2 orange print
☐ light green

Wonder of Egypt (Egypt and Egyptians referred to over 700 times in the Bible). Cut 3 yellow (a), 3 white (b), 3 #1 brown print (b), and 3 gold print (b). Sew white, gold, and brown pieces together, then alternate them with yellow (a) pieces. When hexagon is completed, applique to a 15″ square of gold.

Garden of Eden (Gen. 2:8). Cut 16 yellow print (a), 16 light green (a), 4 #1 brown print (b), and 1 yellow print (c). Sew yellow print (a) and light green (a) into square pictured in each corner of block. Add #1 brown print center strip (b) and attach second square. Make center 1 brown print (b), yellow print (c), and #1 brown print (b). Join three rows.

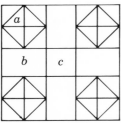
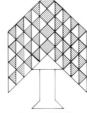

Garden of Eden   *Tree of Life*

Tree of Life (Gen. 2:9). Cut 1 #3 brown print (a), 1 #3 brown print (b), 1 #3 brown print (c), 4 light green (d), 40 light green print (e), and 32 light green (e). Sew leaves together by hand in rows starting at lower left-hand tip. Don't forget to sew (d) to correspond with center of tree. Applique pieced tree to a 15″ white square.

Forbidden Fruit (Gen. 2:15-17). Cut 6 #2 orange print (a), 12 light green print (a), 12 medium green print (a), and 1 #2 brown print (b). Sew leaves together by hand. Scatter apples (#2 orange print). Applique tree to 15″ white block.

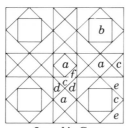

Forbidden Fruit   *Joseph's Coat*

Joseph's Coat (Gen. 37). Cut 5 #2 orange print (a), 4 yellow print (b), 24 orange (c), 16 #2 brown print (d), 16 yellow (e), and 4 white (f). Sew orange (c) triangles to (b) squares. Add yellow (e) pieces to make a square. Four sections are now completed. Sew center sections according to diagram, sewing four center sections first. Make the middle block with the orange (a) piece and 4 white (f) pieces. Sew

this block to two center sections to make a row. Make the top row, one corner square, center section, and another corner square. Make the bottom row the same. Sew each row together.

Rob Peter to Pay Paul (Names are Biblical). Cut 8 #1 orange print (a), 8 yellow (a), 8 #1 orange print (b), and 8 yellow (b). Assemble into four squares as in diagram. Sew the four squares together to make a 15″ block.

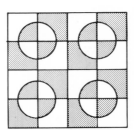
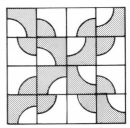

Rob Peter to Pay Paul   *Solomon's Puzzle*

Solomon's Puzzle (I King 3:16-20). Cut 8 medium green print (a), 8 yellow (a), 8 medium green print (b), and 8 yellow (b). This pattern uses the same pieces as the Rob Peter to Pay Paul pattern. Sew one yellow and one green print piece together until there are sixteen small squares. Sew squares together according to chart.

Job's Tears (Job). Cut two 7½″ squares of gold, 4 yellow (a), 4 #3 brown print (a), and 8 gold (b). Alternate colors on four (a) pieces, sewing together at short points. Add four gold (b) pieces to make a square. Sew patchwork squares and solid squares together to form a 15″ block.

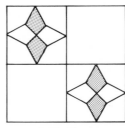
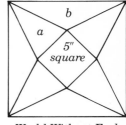

Job's Tears   *World Without End*

World Without End (John 17:3). Lay pattern (b) on fold line of fabric and cut 4 gold pieces, 4 #2 brown print (b), and one 5″ square for the center from #1 orange print. Make a star with (c) piece and 4 (a) pieces. Add the gold (b) pieces.

Jacob's Ladder (Gen. 28:12). Cut 10 light green (a), 10 light green print (a), 4 #1 brown print (b), and 4 light green (b). Make five small squares from (a) pieces as in chart. Make four small squares from pattern (b). Assemble as in chart.

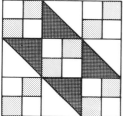
Jacob's Ladder

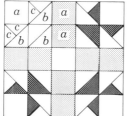
David and Goliath

David and Goliath (I Sam. 17). Cut 8 #2 orange print (a), either 12 #2 orange print (b) or large triangle, 4 #1 brown print (b), 4 light green (a); 8 #1 brown print (c), and 8 light green (c). Make the four corners first with the c and b pieces. Add the (a) square next. Sew center (a) pieces together. Make a row with two corner patchwork squares and 2 (a) pieces to connect them. Make a second row identically. Middle row is 2 orange print, 1 light green, and 2 more orange print pieces. Sew the three rows together.

Steps to Glory (Gen. 28:12). This block is made of sixty-four 1¾″ squares, plus seam allowances. It is another pattern for the Ladder or Stairway to Heaven. The completed block's name is determined by the placement of the colors. You will need 14 gold squares, 22 brown squares, 10 brown dotted squares, and 18 light brown print squares. Join squares according to the diagram.

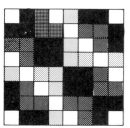
Steps to Glory

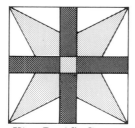
King David's Crown

 gold

▨ brown

▧ brown and white dotted

▩ light brown print

King David's Crown (I Chron. 20:2). Cut 1 #1 orange print (a), 4 #1 orange print (b), 8 orange (c), and 4 #3 brown print (d). Sew the four corners, (c)

and (b) pieces, together first. Connect top row with (d) pieces. Do the same for the bottom row. Sew (d), (a), and (d) pieces together for middle row. Join the three rows.

Step 2. After twenty blocks are finished, cut 5½″ × 15″ strips of brown and sew to the bottom of each block. *This measurement allows ½″ seams.* Below each block on strip, chainstitch name of block with two strands of gold floss.

Step 3. Sew one row of five blocks together. Sew 5½″ × 98″ lattice strips of brown, with right sides of fabric together. If lattice must be pieced, join pieces to match other seams. Be sure to cut all lattice fabric in the same direction to avoid difference in sheen. After all rows are joined, add a 5½″ brown border to top. You may want to chainstitch the quilt's name, your name, and the date across the top. Sew 5½″ brown borders to sides.

Step 4. Iron quilt top. Lay lining, batting, and quilt top on frame. Outline quilting is used throughout quilt. Stitch ¼″ from seams. Stitch through center of each lattice strip once. Stitch along each block seam and around each piece in block pattern. Never allow more than 2″ of unquilted fabric. The heavier the quilting, the more profound the completed project. Use brown quilting thread on brown fabric, gold on gold, and so on.

After quilting is finished, take quilt from frame and baste front and back edges to inside. Stitch in place ¼″ from edges.

Picture Quilt—The Old Swimming Hole

Making pictures from fabric is fun. Anything goes — fanciful and irrational concepts of reality, Abstract Expressionism, or Naturalism. In The Old Swimming Hole, I am striving to make order from the chaos of nature. The beauty of a childhood scene comes before me, and the poison ivy contacted on the excursion is nearly forgotten. This quilt is 45″×54″. I use it as a wall hanging, but it would be ideal for a child's bed. To personalize the quilt, if it is to be a gift, embroider the child's name on the red shirt.

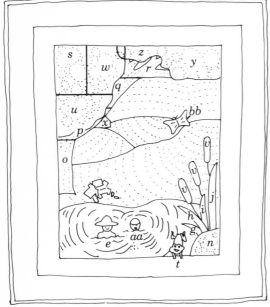

Placement of Old Swimming Hole Quilt shapes (with quilting design)

Materials:

Fabric	Yardage
White with blue flowers	1
Dark blue print	1
Bright blue	1
Green and white dotted	½
Light green	½
Light blue	½
Brown	⅓
Red	⅙
Pink, blue denim, gold dotted, blue print, and gold	⅙
White single-bed sized sheet	
Batting	45″×54″

White quilting thread	1 spool
Embroidery floss:	
Red, gold, blue, white, variegated green, black, and dark green	1 skein each

Method:

Step 1. *Background.* Cut light blue sky 14″×30″, green grass 18″×30″, and bright blue water 14″×30″. Round the green hills slightly and do the same with the water to avoid a "straight line" landscape. Stitch grass to sky with a hidden applique stitch. Do the same with the water, overlapping the grass. Press and trim background to measure 30″×40″.

Step 2. *Picture pieces.* Using freezer paper make pattern of tree trunk and limbs (o, p, q, r) by joining o and p at three notches, p and q at singe notch, and r and q at four notches. Cut brown tree trunk and limbs, adding seam allowance. Pin to background.

Make pattern for tree leaves (s, u, w, y, z) by joining s and u at two notches, w and s at three notches, and z and y at nocthes. Cut from green and white dotted fabric and pin into place.

Cut a barn (x) from red fabric and a silo (c) from light blue. Pin barn behind tree and silo behind barn. Applique all pieces into place.

Cut out blue denim shorts (m), blue print shirt (b), red shirt (a), and layer into a not-so-neat pile and applique. Place gold dotted (bb) butterfly along the horizon and applique. Cut pink children's bodies (faces e and aa; shoulders f), line with white. Pin into place. Give girl a gold straw hat (d) and applique around all pieces.

Cut brown rock (n) and three brown cattails (v). Cut green and white dotted cattail leaves (g, i, h, j, j). Join the two (j) pieces at notches to make pattern. Slightly stuff cattails as you applique.

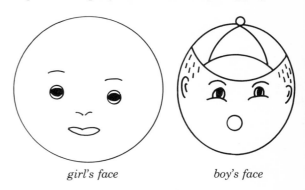

girl's face   *boy's face*

Step 3. *Embroidery details.* These make a picture quilt exceptional. Give children facial features, including black pupils in their eyes. Use French knots for pupils and for buttons on the print shirt. Fill boy's hat with red and blue chainstitches.

straw hat

Chainstitch around straw hat with gold floss. Chainstitch water movement with blue. Chainstitch variegated green frog (t). Make a blue pupil in the frog's eye with solid stitches, and chainstitch around the eye with white floss. Chainstitch the

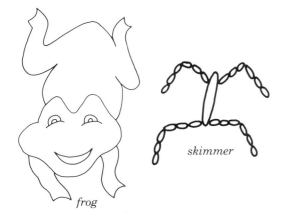

skimmer

frog

frog's red mouth. Add a black skimmer (l) to water. Satinstitch its black body and chainstitch its black legs. Embroider a scattering of gold dandelions along bank with several straight stitches crossed in center. Add outline of chainstitches on short's seam lines and pockets. Do the same on shirts with pockets, collars, and ribbing. Make blue satin-

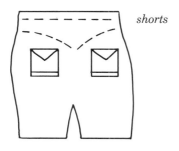

shorts

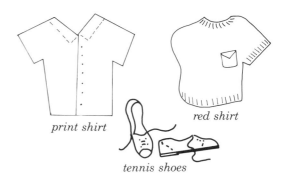

print shirt

red shirt

tennis shoes

stitched tennis shoes (k) look almost real with white backstitches. Outline tree trunk with brown chainstitches, and butterfly with gold. Satinstitch barn windows and backstitch barn door with white floss.

butterfly

barn

There is a field of hay in the background. The neatly contoured windrows are shown with green floss in herringbone stitches. With same green, make short stitches around tree and along water to represent blades of grass.

Step 4. *Borders.* Cut 2 bright blue strips 48″ × 5″ and 2 strips 38″ × 5″. With right sides of fabric together, pin borders to quilt sides and ends, with 4″ extending from ends. Miter corners. Sew border around entire scene. The second border is done in the same way. Cut white print into two 56″ × 5″ and two 46″ × 5″ strips. Sew strips to bright blue print border.

Step 5. *Quilting.* Cut 45″ × 54″ lining piece from a sheet and lay on a table. Cut batting the same size, then quilt top to lining. Start at center and baste out to the edge in spokes. Do this at least twelve times. This will keep layers together for easy lap quilting, which I suggest because of the curved lines in the quilting. I like to use an oval quilting frame for the center picture and no frame at all for quilting the borders.

In a picture quilt, quilting is a great part of the overall design. It adds texture to surfaces of objects in the frame as well as serving the traditional function of securing three layers of fabric together.

Mark stitching lines with a dressmaker's chalk pencil. Do only a couple lines at a time, as they rub off quite easily. If you quilt on a large square frame, however, the entire quilt can be marked at once.

Start with the hayfield, stitching next to the embroidered herringbone stitches. Quilt along each row of hay and each side. The green grass pasture is also quilted on the contour. In field next to water, start at top of hill, quilting around it at ½″ intervals, gradually increasing width until quilting is 1″ apart to create the illusion of distance. In yard around barn, quilt in ¼″ rows. The field behind tree is quilted in rows ½″ apart that taper as they arrive at hilltop.

Texture of tree trunk is determined by narrow rows of quilting, which follow lines of tree. Leaves are circles graduated from ½″ to 1¾″ in diameter.

Quilt tiny square cement blocks in silo. Water movement in pond is quilted along embroidered lines. Texture in rock is quilted half-circles, which are about the size of a quarter. Quilt around inside of cattail leaves. Quilt sky with horizon line at 1″ intervals.

Quilt border entirely around quilt ¼″ from the first border seam. Make another round in center of first border, a third round ¼″ from second border seam, and a fourth round in center of second border.

Step 6. Make 6 yards of bright blue tape. It need not be on the bias for straight edges. Cut strips 2″ wide and press in half. Place right side of tape to right side of quilt and sew a ¼″ seam. Miter corners. Blindstitch hem on back of lining.

Seminole Patchwork

Little is known about the Seminoles, but we do know they include remnants of the Creek, Hitchiti, and Yuchi tribes. They first used the name Seminole about 1775. It means "separationist" or "runaway" in the Cree language. They fled to Florida, away from relentless pursuit by U.S. troops. In 1835 the federal government attempted to move the Seminoles to the West, which resulted in the costliest Indian war of the decade. Thousands of Indians and 1,500 soldiers died. Seven generals failed to subdue the Seminoles while they were led by the famous Osceola, but some were marched to Oklahoma where their descendants live still. Others escaped into the Florida swamps and Everglades. Today about 1,150 Seminoles live in Florida. They have accepted white inventions and education, but they cherish their own tradition.

Mary Matlow, a skilled craftswoman relates how the Seminoles acquired their first European fabric. She said that heavily laden ships sailing along the coast of Florida had to jettison cargo to avoid dangerous coral reefs. Some of the cargo was rolls of fabric, and the Seminole women collected them from the beach, took them home, and made clothing.

No one is sure when or where the unique Seminole patchwork idea was first conceived, but some speculate that the basic concept was adopted from early American colonists and expanded to the variety of colorful patterns we are familiar with today.

One of the first descriptions of Seminole clothing was made by a white man who visited the Indian villages in 1880. That description sounds very much like a current description, because then, as now, both men and women wore clothing ornamented with bright appliqued strips of colored cloth. Often a single strip of geometric designs is attached near the bottom of shirts and skirts.

The Seminoles have preserved much of their heritage. Traditional flowing dresses and capes continue to be popular. Mary Matlow tells of learning to sew patchwork at an early age. Now, she says, "I make a design in my mind and then apply it to the cloth." She says women do not "own" patterns, and they exchange ideas. Trading new patterns and adding to a collection is part of the fun of patchwork.

Mary Matlow is talented, and she demonstrates patchwork in Okalee Village, a village in Hollywood, Florida, that is authentically recreated to present to the public the Seminole way of life.

Seminole patchwork is a challenging craft. The width of the solid strips, the number of solid strips joined, their colors, the angle at which they are cut apart, and the manner in which they are rejoined offer endless possibilities. Lightweight cottons and blends are ideal for Seminole patchwork. Durable denims are used in large designs. Satins, with their illusion of luxury, remain a favorite for accessories. Velvets, velours, and wools accommodate large patterns in wall hangings and quilts.

Mixing of colors and designs are individual choices. Combining prints and solids is popular in contemporary Seminole patchwork. After patchwork bands are completed, the addition of commercial trims like old-fashioned rickrack may appeal to some. This trim promotes the look of original Seminole design. Some traditional and contemporary Seminole designs follow, all with ¼" seam allowances.

A single traditional zigzag design is made by sewing three strips of fabric together. They may be of

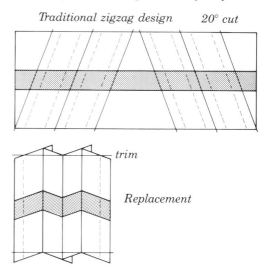

Traditional zigzag design   *20° cut*

trim

Replacement

any width but the top and bottom strips must be much wider than the finished band when using a diagonal cut. A ½" finished strip must be cut 1" wide to allow for ¼" seams. The diagonal may be cut at any angle, but the angle should be identical in any one pattern. The sharper the angle, the more pointed the design. A 20° angle will produce a smooth zigzag. This design is a double diagonal cut.

The zigzag may also be varied by cutting wide or narrow segments from the strips. A narrow cut gives more numerous points in a single zigzag pattern. It is also possible to make several zigzag patterns at the same time by sewing several strips together. Combine stripes with solids, prints, pastels, and darks to make an interesting band.

After the first three strips are sewn together, press. Mark on back of the patchwork fabric, the cut lines for replacement pieces, in a double diagonal pattern. To do this start with the left lower corner and measure and mark toward the center of the fabric. Start again at the lower right corner and mark diagonal lines to the left until the right and left lines meet at the center. Be sure to allow ¼″ seam allowance for all pieces. Carefully cut out marked pieces on the cut lines. Baste the pieces together, matching seams to encourage a smooth design; place alternating left cut, right cut in a vertical position. Sew replacement pieces together securely either by hand or machine. I find narrow, small patterns are easier to do by hand. The larger wide designs can be done by machine. After sewing, press and trim off top and bottom excess material.

A traditional one-pattern band in sawtooth design is made with three strips of fabric sewn together. The

Traditional sawtooth design (one-pattern band)

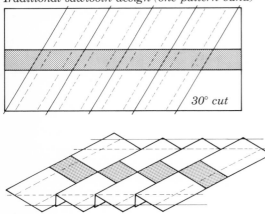

30° cut

two outside strips are wider than the center strip. Any width strips may be used. Contemporary Seminoles use narrow 2″ and 3″ bands more than they do wider bands. The strips are cut at a 30° angle and sewn in the replacement arrangement diagonally. This is a single diagonal cut. A variation of this pattern is made by cutting wider strips for replacement.

The double sawtooth pattern is made by sewing five strips together and using a single diagonal cut for

Traditional double sawtooth design (one-pattern band)

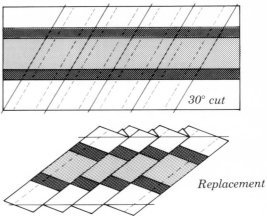

30° cut

Replacement

replacement. Triple sawtooth designs may also be made in this manner. A one-pattern band can look complicated if begun with more and narrower strips.

Traditional two-pattern bands are made in the same way as one-pattern bands, except that two separate patterns are pieced, cut, and replaced in a common band. I do not give measurements because bands can be made as wide or as narrow as desired.

In A, the two patterns are separated with a plain strip. The straight cut is the width of the center strip

Traditional two-pattern band design   A

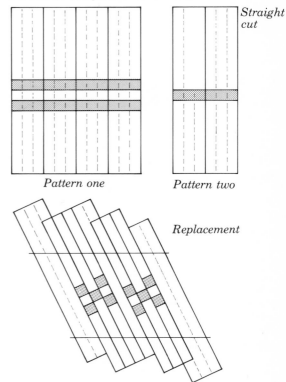

Straight cut

Pattern one

Pattern two

Replacement

plus seam allowances.

In B, the center strip in pattern 2 is four times the width of the center strip in pattern 1 plus seam allowances. The straight cut width is equal to the

B

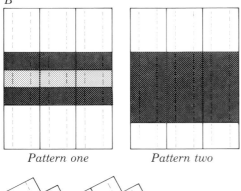

Pattern one   Pattern two

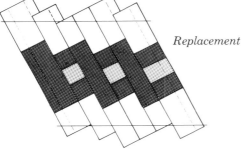

Replacement

center strip in the first pattern plus seam allowances. Alternating strips are replaced diagonally.

The center strip in pattern one, C, is ⅓ the width of that in pattern two. Straight cut width equals the

C

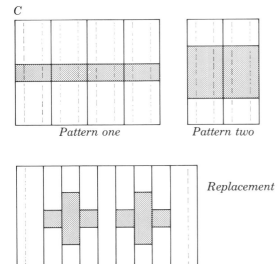

Pattern one   Pattern two

Replacement

center strip of pattern 1 plus seam allowances. Replace alternating strips separated by plain strips vertically.

The straight cut in D, pattern 1, equals the width of the second strip plus seam allowance. The straight cut in D, pattern 2, equals the width plus seam allowance of the third or dark strip in pattern 1.

D

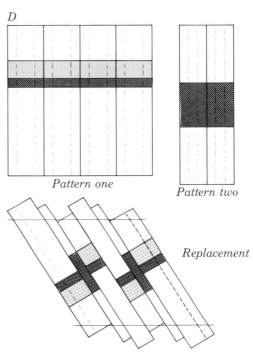

Pattern one   Pattern two

Replacement

Traditional three-pattern bands are the most difficult to make because you sew three different patterns first, which are then cut and replaced in a new common band. The difficulty is remembering the order, so keep the pattern before you as you sew. These designs are used extensively on Seminole clothing.

Traditional three-pattern band designs

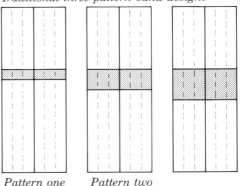

Pattern one   Pattern two

33

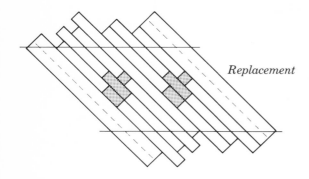

Replacement

Three-pattern bands are separated with a plain strip in the common band in these *two* patterns.

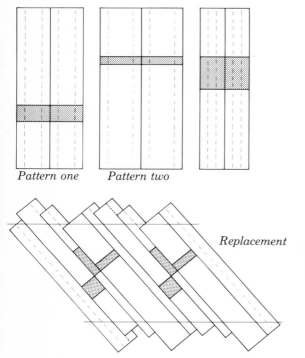

Pattern one   *Pattern two*

Replacement

Contemporary chevron design

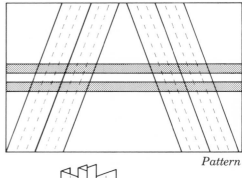

Pattern

Replacement

Contemporary plaid design

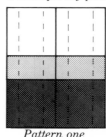

Pattern one   *Pattern two*

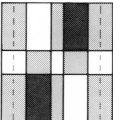

Replacement

The contemporary chevron design is made from one pattern of five strips. The strips are cut double diagonal. Remember to make top and bottom strips wide enough to allow for the diagonal cut. The three inside strips are the same width. Variations of replacement develop new patterns. The design shown uses straight replacement, alternating two right cuts, two left cuts, etc..

Plaids are made from two patterns. The center strips of the two patterns are the same width. Cut and replacement determine design of the band. Reverse

pattern one between pattern two. The design shown uses straight cut and straight replacement.

For simple squares, cut an even number of strips the same width and sew together. Vary the colors and patterns of fabric, keeping in mind a central color scheme. Cut the pattern vertically the same width, plus seam allowance the width of the strips. Vary design in replacement. Segments are arranged in a vertically alternating fashion. Try reversing rows 2 and 4 in the horizontal arrangement.

Simple squares

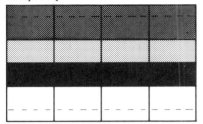

Pattern

Replacement variations

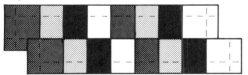

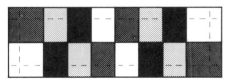

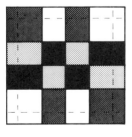

Handkerchief Print Pillow

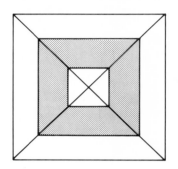

Materials:

Fabric	Yardage
#1 (light print)	1
#2 (dark print)	¼

Method:

Step 1. Cut fabric #1, following layout and making strips 60″ × 3″; 60″ × 2″; 90″ × 6″ for ruffle, and a 14½″ square for back. Cut fabric #2, making strip 60″ × 3½″.

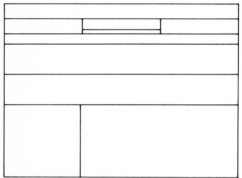

Step 1. Cutting layout, fabric #1

Step 2. Sew 60″ pieces together to make a striped design with dark print in center. Piece will be 7½″ wide after joining.

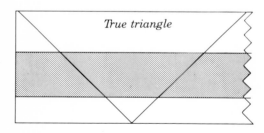

True triangle

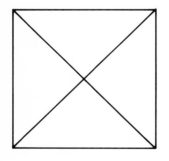

Step 3. On wrong side of fabric trace four true triangles, placing hypotenuse of triangle template on length of fabric. Cut and join triangles, carefully matching all seams.

Step. 4. Make ruffle by sewing ends of 6″ wide strips together in continuous loop. Fold in half lengthwise, wrong sides together, and press. Mark into four equal lengths with pins. In each section make two rows of machine-basting gathering threads slightly inside the ½″ seam allowance.

Step 5. Pin ungathered ruffle to right side of pillow front, matching raw edges of ruffle to raw edges of pillow front. Ruffle will extend toward center of pillow front. Gather each ruffle section to fit pillow side, allowing extra fullness at corners. Baste all thicknesses together.

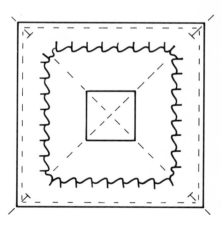

Step 6. Pin 14½″ square pillow back to pillow front and ruffle unit, right sides of fabric together. Sew three sides, trim corners, and turn right side out. Stuff with polyester fiber or a pillow and hand stitch the remaining side closed.

Seminole Patchwork Pillow
One-pattern sawtooth band

Materials:

Fabric	Yardage
#1 (blue and white striped)	$\frac{1}{3}$
#2 (red and white checked)	$\frac{1}{8}$
#3 (white)	1
Pillow form (or filling)	16″ square

Method:

Step 1. Cut fabric #1, making two $32'' \times 5''$ strips. Cut fabric #2, making one $32'' \times 1\frac{1}{2}''$ strip.

Step 2. Sew strips together lengthwise with fabric #2 in center and press. Finished piece will be $10\frac{1}{2}''$ wide.

Step 3. On wrong side of band mark 30° diagonal lines $1\frac{1}{2}''$ apart and cut.

Step 4. Sew together, lowering diamond of fabric #2 to form double diamond pattern. (See photograph in color section.) Trim excess fabric from top and bottom. The band will be $7'' \times 16''$.

Step 5. Cut fabric #3, making two $3'' \times 16''$ strips. Sew to top and bottom of band.

Step 6. Cut fabric #2, making two $2\frac{1}{2}'' \times 16''$ strips. Sew to top and bottom of band.

Step 7. Make ruffle by cutting fabric #3 into four $26'' \times 2\frac{1}{2}''$ strips. Sew together in continuous loop.

Turn $\frac{1}{4}''$ under twice and sew hem on one side of loop. Mark into four equal lengths with pins. In each section make two rows of machine-basting gathering threads.

Step 8. Pin ungathered ruffle to pillow front, right sides of fabric together, with each section on one side of pillow. Gather each ruffle section to fit pillow side, allowing extra fullness at corners. Baste all thicknesses together.

Step. 9. Make envelope-type back. Cut two $16'' \times 10''$ pieces fabric #3. Hem one 16″ edge on each piece. Pin unhemmed back edges to pillow top, right sides of fabric together, with back pieces overlapping to form an envelope closure. Stitch through all thicknesses. Doublestitch where back pieces overlap.

Step 10. Trim corners and turn case right side out. Fill with pillow.

Seminole Patchwork Shopping Bag
Double sawtooth design

Materials:

Fabric	Yardage
#1 (red denim)	1½
#2 (red print)	2″
#3 (bright blue print)	2″
#4 (blue and white striped)	6″
#5 (white)	2″

Method:

Step 1. Cut fabric #2, making two 1″ × 40″ strips. Cut fabric #3, making one 2″ × 40″ strips. Cut fabric #4, making two 3″ × 40″ strips.

Step 2. Sew together to make band, with strips of fabric in this order: #4, #2, #3, #2, and #4. Press.

Step 3. On wrong side of band mark 30° diagonals 1″ apart and cut.

Step 4. Sew together, with strips forming a row of red diamonds, a row of bright blue zigzag, and another row of red diamonds. (See photograph in color section.) Seams are ¼″.

Step 5. Make shopping bag pattern by cutting brown paper grocery bag down one corner and around bottom to produce two pattern pieces.

Step 6. Cut 20″ × 39″ bag, 13″ × 8″ bag bottom, and two 14″ × 8″ handles from fabric #1. Sew handles with right sides of fabric together, turn, and press. Using crease marks of brown bag as a guide (dotted lines), press folds in large bag piece. Pin Seminole band to center front. Cut two 1″ × 20″ strips fabric #5 and fold under edges. Baste to edge of Seminole band and sew in place as finishing edge. Pin handles to bag top with front handle ends on each side of Seminole band and back handle ends corresponding. Cut 39″ × 2″ facing strip of fabric #1, turn up raw edge and stitch. Pin remaining raw edge to bag top, right sides of fabric together. Stitch ½″ seam.

Step 7. Pin bottom to bag, right sides of fabric together, and stitch ½″ *seam twice*. Pin ½″ side seam and stitch up through facing, clip intercepting seams and press.

Step 8. Turn bag right side out. Fold facing to inside and press. Topstitch edge.

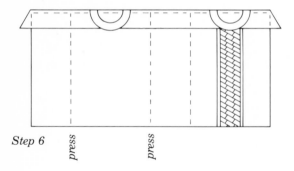

Step 6   *press*   *press*

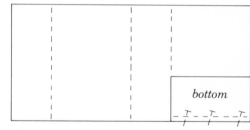

bottom

Step 7

Seminole Patchwork Apron
Two-pattern band

Materials:

Fabric	Yardage
#1 (red denim)'	1
#2 (blue and white striped)	⅔
#3 (navy print)	⅛
#4 (red and white checked)	⅛

Method:

Step 1. Make pattern one for Seminole band. Cut fabric #2, making two 3½″×24″ strips and one 1½″×24″ strip. Cut fabric #3, making two 1½″×24″ strips. Sew together as follows: wide fabric #2 strip, #3 strip, narrow #2 strip, #3 strip, and wide #2 strip. Press.

Step 2. Make pattern two for Seminole band. Cut fabric #2, making two 5″×45″ strips. Cut fabric #4, making one 1½″×45″ strip. Sew together as follows: fabric #2 strip, #4 strip, and #2 strip. Press.

Step 3. Mark wrong side both patterns on the vertical 1½″ apart. This allows for ¼″ seam allowances. Cut.

Step 4. Cut fabric #2, making 1½″×24″ strip. Replace pieces into new pattern as follows: 1 strip pattern one, 1 strip pattern two, 1 strip pattern one, and 1 strip fabric #2. This last strip separates the completed designs. Continue replacement to make six complete designs. (See photograph in color section.)

Step 5. Press band. Trim excess fabric from top and bottom. Add piece fabric #2 at each end to square band. Finished band is 5½″×34″.

Step 6. Cut apron. Cut fabric #1, making 18″×34″ skirt, 6″×20″ waistband, two 24″×4″ ties, and 6″×6″ pocket. Press 1″ hem on skirt bottom.

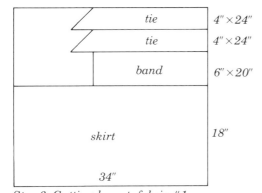

tie	4″×24″
tie	4″×24″
band	6″×20″
skirt	18″
34″	

Step 6. Cutting layout, fabric #1

Step 7. Apply Seminole band to skirt. Fold under edges of band. Press. Pin band to skirt 1″ from bottom and sew, catching apron hem at same time. Pin top band to skirt. Sew.

gather line

topstitch

hem

Step 7

Step 8. Finish apron. Hem skirt sides ½″. Stitch two rows machine-basting gathering threads at top. Gather skirt to fit waistband less seam allowances of ½″ at each side. Pin right sides of fabric together and sew, leaving seam allowances at ends. Hem edges of ties ¼″, pin to waistband, and sew. (Seam allowances will be hidden in waistband.) Press top of waistband to inside and sew to skirt on inside. Make 1″ hem on top pocket and press ½″ under on remaining three edges. Pin pocket to right-hand side apron skirt and sew.

press
sew

Step 8

Checkerboard Pillow (20″ square)
Simple squares design

Materials:

Fabric	Yardage
#1 (red)	⅓
#2 (navy blue)	1
Navy zipper	12″
Pillow form (optional)	20″ square
Plastic checkers (optional)	

Method:

Step 1. Cut fabric #1, making four 2½″ × 24″ strips. Cut fabric #2, making four 2½″ × 24″ strips. Sew together, alternating colors. Press.

Step 2. Mark wrong side on the vertical 2½″ apart. Cut.

Step 3. Replace, alternating colors, with four red and four blue squares in each row. Finished size is 16½″ square. (See simple squares design earlier in chapter.)

Step 4. Finish pillow-gameboard top. Cut fabric #2, making four 2½″ × 20½″ strips. Frame checkerboard by pinning one strip to each side, right sides of fabric together. Sew, mitering corners.

Step 5. Make back. Cut fabric #2, making two 10½″ × 20″ pieces. Stitch seam, right sides of fabric together, on 20″ edges. Install 12″ zipper in seam.

Step. 6. Pin checkerboard and back, right sides of fabric together. Stitch seam. Turn through zipper opening. Stuff with pillow form or checkers for use as children's travel game.

Glasses Case
Three-pattern band

Materials:

Fabric	Yardage
#1 (white)	1/12
#2 (blue)	⅓
#3 (red)	1/12
White flannel or batting	8″ square
White lining (if batting used)	8″ square
Red grosgrain ribbon, ½″ wide	½ yd.

Method:

Step 1. Make pattern one for Seminole band. Cut fabric #1, making one 1″ × 12″ strip. Cut fabric #2, making one 3½″ × 12″ strip and one 5″ × 12″ strip. Place white strip in center and sew strips together with ¼″ seams. Press.

Step 2. Make pattern two for Seminole band. Cut fabric #2, making one 3½″ × 12″ strip and one 5″ × 12″ strip. Cut fabric #3, making one 1½″ × 12″ strip. Place red strip in center and sew together. Press.

Step 3. Make pattern three for Seminole band. Cut fabric #2, making one 3½″ × 12″ strip and one 5″ × 12″ strip. Cut fabric #3, making one ¾″ × 12″ strip. Press.

Step 4. Mark wrong side pattern one on the vertical 1″ apart. Cut. Mark wrong side pattern two on the vertical ¾″ apart. Cut. Mark wrong side pattern three on the vertical 1¼″ apart. Cut. Cut fabric #2, making four 1¼″ × 10″ strips.

Step 5. Replace pieces into new pattern as follows: plain blue strip, pattern one, pattern two, pattern three, plain blue. This last strip separates com-

pleted designs. Continue replacement to complete three designs. Press. Trim to finished 4″ × 8″ size. (See three-pattern design earlier in chapter.)

Step 6. Cut fabric #2, making 4″ × 8″ rectangle for case back. Right sides together, join case back and front on left 8″ edges. Cut 8″ square flannel or batting. Lay right side up on wrong side of patchwork if flannel is used. If batting is used, cut 8″ square of lining and lay right side up on batting. Sew layers together on left-hand 8″ edge.

Step 7. Cut strip 1½″ × 8″ facing for top edge case. Stitch ½″ hem on one edge. Pin raw edge to case, right sides of fabric facing, and sew.

Step 8. Fold case with right sides of patchwork and back together and sew bottom and side. Trim corners. Turn.

Step 9. Hand-stitch facing in place on top inside lining. Turn case right side out.

Step 10. Tack red ribbon to inside case. Hang case around neck.

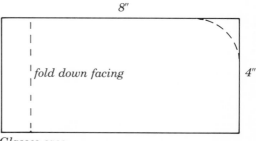

Glasses case

Hoop De-Do Series: Patchwork Portraiture

The Hoop De-Do Series is a collection of fabric portraits for beginners as well as more experienced craftspersons. If you can stitch a straight line and stuff a sock, you can master Spotty Dog, Digger in the hot air balloon. The background is only one color and soft sculpture is not difficult.

And it's a delightful way to capture memories. Spotty Dog, Digger, for instance, was a small white dog that loved to give muddy attention to his owner, my cousin Corrin, and me when we were grade-school children. If we had had a hot air balloon, we would have sent him to the moon! In the Clearing recalls the quieter joy of watching through binoculars as a doe raised her fawn one summer. The nostalgia of Saturday Night may prompt grandparents to tell stories of the "good old days" — especially if you personalize the bather by adding more or different-colored hair or by embroidering a name on the towel.

You can also create a currently meaningful picture. Sleeping Peasants grew from Picasso's *Sleeping Peasants*. Milk and Honey is an original abstract expression of Exodus 3:8, with browns to represent bread, gold for honey, and white for milk. Imagine the 14″ block as the land producing these life-sustaining foods.

All the Hoop De-Do Series combine quilting, patchwork, embroidery, and soft sculpture. In fact, they are soft — soft so the figures will not stand out from the background in an unnatural stance in most instances. The strawberries in the Bunny in the Berry Patch are exceptions. They are packed tightly with fiber to retain their shape and appear plump, ripe, and ready to eat. A very soft strawberry, if you recall, is dark, almost brown, squishy to the touch, and not tasty. Green berries, in reality, are even more solid than the red fruit. If realism is your goal add a half-eaten berry and a few little black bugs!

But in my fabric art, I dwell on the beauty of our surroundings and eliminate the trash. The only time I find use for including the mundane is in a picture created for humorous or comic purposes.

I find there is no limit to what can be done with fabric, although soft scenes are my favorites. And although they are "soft," they do have texture. The fabric chosen for a project determines the texture to some degree. Coarsely woven, nubby, or sheer fabrics

— all make a statement. More texture may be added by embroidery. French knots, chainstitches, or satin stitches add interest to a surface. And texture is also added by quilting. Sun rays, for instance, can radiate across the sky horizontally or vertically. The terrain, or texture of grass and soil, is created by quilting in designs. In Rise and Shine, the green background is quilted in the line of the horizon. For In the Clearing, the grass is quilted in half-round humps to resemble bunchgrass.

Texture adds clarity and aesthetic value to the expression of ideas with fabric. In museums or art exhibits notice how texture is used in sculpture. Some pieces are smooth as silk and others are rough and ragged. Often there is a combination of textures in one piece. Surprisingly, there are innumerable degrees of texture in fabric, perhaps not as pronounced as those in materials such as wood, metal, and marble, but noticeable, nonetheless.

If a project will never be washed, experiment with combinations. Use fake fur for animals, silk for flowers, and dotted swiss for a star-studded night sky.

I have used cotton and cotton-polyester blends exclusively in this chapter for practical reasons. However, I believe each scene may be as elaborate or as simple as the reader pleases.

Now a few lines about stuffing the soft figures in the following pieces. Don't grab a handful of polyester fill, scrunch it up the size of a baseball, and jab it into the body. If you do, don't expect shapely results. The trick is to take small wads of fiber and push them into corners with a pencil or crochet hook. When the corner is firmly but softly filled, add several more clumps of fiber until the form is full. If you want the object to stand up and look you in the eye, pack the stuffing tightly and solidly.

The basic structure of the Hoop De-Do Series is lining, batting, background, and additional scenery and shapes. The background material is turned over the lining on the back side and stitched down to form a casing. To hold the picture taut, run elastic or a drawstring through the casing. Pull fabric smooth but not too tight, which would make it difficult to quilt. The scene can then be hung on the wall in a 22″ circular wooden quilting hoop. The hoops can be purchased at quilt shops and many fabric and craft stores.

Spotty Dog, Digger

Materials:

Fabric	Yardage
Light blue	2 square yards
Gold	⅛
Pink	⅛
Green	⅛
Brown	⅛
White	⅛
Bright blue	⅓
Embroidery floss:	
Black, red, and dark blue	1 skein each
Batting	1½
Pink ribbon, ½" wide	⅓
White quilting thread	1 spool
Elastic, ½" wide	40"
Polyester fiber	
22" round quilt hoop	

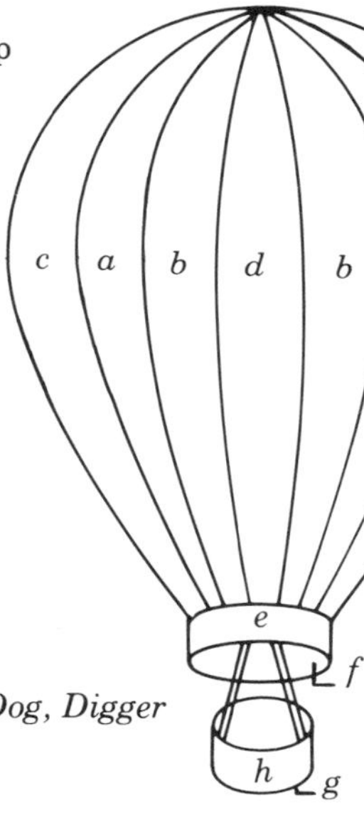

Placement, Spotty Dog, Digger

Method:

Step 1. Make background and lining of two 36" circles from light blue fabric. Cut batting in a 30" circle. Stack layers with batting in middle and baste across circle in two places, dividing circle into four equal sections. Trim ¾" from lining. Fold background fabric over lining, fold under ¼", and baste. This forms casing for the elastic. Sew casing with sewing machine, leaving small opening to insert elastic. Run elastic through casing with the help of a safety pin. Tack ends of elastic together.

Step 2. Place background in hoop and smooth fabric.

Step 3. Mark quilting pattern of sky background by first measuring circle into eighths and placing a straight pin for each section at edge of hoop. Now wrap a thread around one pin and stretch to opposite pin and wrap again. Quilt from center to edge along these lines. (Another method of marking is to draw lines with dressmaker's chalk. If you use chalk, remember that it rubs off easily. You will be removing the fabric from the hoop to replace marks and wasting much time.) If you plan to display this scene in an oblong hoop, extend quilting lines out to elastic.

Step 4. Make balloon. Cut 1 green (d), 2 gold (a), 2 pink (b), and 2 bright blue (c) with ¼" seam allowance. Baste together, matching notches. Sew. Cut 1 bright blue (e) and baste to bottom of balloon. Press balloon and use as a pattern to cut lining and batting the same size. Lay lining right side up on batting, then balloon wrong side up. Pin pieces together and sew leaving the bottom open. Cut 1 bright blue (f). Baste edges under and pin to bottom of balloon. Handstitch in place. Cut two 6" lengths of ribbon. Fold each in half and tack to inside of balloon bottom. Quilt along balloon seams to give illusion of inflation.

Step 5. Make balloon basket. Cut 1 strip brown 4" × 10" (h). Sew ends together. Cut strip batting 2" × 10". Place batting on wrong side of brown. Fold center of brown down to cover batting. Baste bottom edges together. Cut 2 brown (g) basket bottoms. Baste sides and bottom together and sew in place. Quilt two rows around basket sides and one circle in bottom. Tack basket to ribbon so it hangs evenly.

Step 6. Make Spotty Dog, Digger. Draw dog (i) on wrong side of white fabric. Place another piece of the same fabric on top, right sides of fabric together. Pin. Sew, leaving a 2" opening at bottom. Cut out dog with a ¼" seam allowance. Clip seams, turn, and stuff with batting. Sew bottom seam. Embroider black eye, nose, and spots and red mouth using satin stitches.

Embroidery guide, dog

Step 7. Place balloon on sky. Tack to background, stitching through all layers of background at top of balloon and 2" down on both sides. The basket or gondola hangs freely. Put the dog in the basket and hang the picture in a child's room.

Bunny in the Berry Patch

Materials:

Fabric	Yardage
White	2 sq. yd.
Green print	½
Dark green	½
Red	½
Brown	⅓
Green	6″ square
Gold	⅓
Embroidery floss:	
Blue, black, red, and gold	1 skein each
Batting	1 sq. yd.
Elastic, ½″ wide	40″
White quilting thread	1 spool
Polyester fiber	
Thread to match all fabrics	1 spool each
22″ quilt hoop	

Method:

Step 1. Cut two 36″ circles from white fabric for background and lining. Cut 30″ circle from batting. Cut 11″ × 18″ rectangle from green print for grass. Round 18″ side to correspond with 22″ quilt hoop. Curve top edge for horizon. Pin green print to background, leaving a 1½″ white border around side and bottom. Lay lining, batting, and background together. Applique green print in place. Trim ¾″ from edge of lining and fold background fabric over lining. Turn under a narrow hem to form casing for the elastic. Insert elastic and tack ends together.

Step 2. Pull fabric layers over quilt hoop, smooth wrinkles, and tighten hoop.

Step 3. Quilt 3 rows ½″ apart around entire circle. This gives a border effect. Quilt across grass twice, with evenly spaced rows, following contour of horizon.

Step 4. Cut 7″ circle from gold fabric for sun. Press ¼″ hem under and applique to upper right corner. Quilt sun with 4 rows of stitches ½″ apart. Quilt around sun on background, stopping at border in background.

Step 5. Make calyx for tops of berries. Small pieces, such as the star-shaped caylx, are much easier to make if sewn together before being cut out. Pin two layers of green fabric together. Draw around caylx pattern (a). Make 10. Follow marks when sewing. Leave a small opening for turning. Cut out calyx and trim excess fabric from points. Turn and close opening.

Step 6. Make berries. Cut 8 red strawberries (f) plus seam allowances. Fold right sides of fabric together in center of dotted line. Sew half-circle together on straight edges. Leave a small opening for turning.

Turn right side out and baste gathering thread around curved edge. Stuff berry until firm and draw up gathering thread tightly. Stitch top shut and tack calyx on top of berry, covering gathering. Cut 2 smaller green berries (c) and complete in the same manner. Using gold embroidery floss, make 12 French knots on each berry for achenes, or seeds.

Step 7. Make leaves. Cut 18 dark green leaves (d). Sew two leaves together, right sides of fabric together, leaving a small opening for turning. Turn and sew opening shut. Make 9 leaves. Place three to a plant on grass. Sew up center of each leaf through all thickness of background to within ½″ from tip. Tips of leaves will tend to curve upward.

Step 8. Attach berries with a double strand of green thread to center of calyx. Draw thread through center of strawberry plant and shorten until 1″ to 1½″ stem is visible. Secure thread. Berries will dangle from plant like real fruit.

Step 9. Make bunny. Cut 2 bunny bodies (e). Sew together, leaving top neck edge open for turning. Turn and stuff lightly. Stitch across dotted line to sculpt form. Tack on a ball of batting for a cotton tail. Cut 2 bunny heads (f) and sew together, stuffing lightly following method used for body. Satinstitch solid dark blue eyes and a black nose. Chainstitch a red smile. With short running stitches and white quilting thread, stitch around eyes and in ears for shading effect. Sew head to body. Tack complete bunny to corner of berry patch.

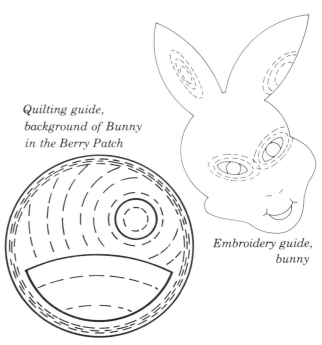

Quilting guide, background of Bunny in the Berry Patch

Embroidery guide, bunny

Saturday Night

The basic color of this Saturday Night is pink because that goes well with our first-floor bathroom. Find a couple of prints that fit into your color scheme. Make the stove and its doors from solid colors that appear in the prints. The stovepipe and legs could be black, gray, or navy. Test the prints and solids for compatibility before you cut fabric. Create a picture for your private use — and may you enjoy every moment of it.

Materials:

Fabric	Yardage
Batting	1 sq. yd.
Lining	1 sq. yd.
Flowered print (wallpaper)	⅔
Contrasting print (linoleum)	⅓
Deep pink (stove)	⅓
Light blue, navy, green, white, red and white striped, light pink, and brown	⅙ each
Embroidery floss:	
White, red, black, and brown	1 skein each
White quilting thread	1 spool
Elastic, ½" wide	40"
Polyester fiber	
22" quilt hoop	

Method:

Step 1. Make background. Sew wallpaper print and linoleum print together. Press and cut a 36" circle. Also cut a 36" circle from lining and a 30" circle from batting. Cut 36"x1" white strip, press ¼" hems on edges, and sew strip over seam connecting two prints. Pin lining, batting, and background together. Trim ¾" from lining, fold under a ¼" hem, and sew. This is casing for elastic. Insert elastic and tack ends together.

Step 2. Place background in hoop and smooth.

Step 3. Hand-quilt vertical lines 1½" apart across wallpaper. Quilt horizontal lines 1½" apart across floor.

Step 4. Cut deep pink stove (a), fold under edges ¼", and applique onto background. Add navy legs (e) and navy (h) stovepipe. Cut 4 small green doors (b) and 1 large door (c). Place 2 warming oven doors horizontally on upper part of stove. Place 2 more doors vertically on lower part of stove. Separate them with larger green oven door. Applique.

Step 5. Quilt three rows ¼" apart below warming ovens. Chainstitch with white floss along bottom of warming oven doors. Chainstitch ¼" below quilting with black floss to designate the cooking surface. Applique a light blue teapot (g) to burner surface. Quilt small, steamlike stitches coming out of spout. Applique a white woodbox (c) near stove. (Woodbox uses same pattern as large oven door.) Quilt vertical lines of lumber used to make woodbox. Embroider brown sticks of wood in box. Embroider white handles on stove doors, white and chrome under cooking surface, black handle on teapot, and black draft control on stovepipe. Use outline, satin, or chain stitches. (See photograph in color section.)

Step 6. Cut a red and white striped towel (f), fringe edge, and tack to oven door handle.

Step 7. Cut 2 brown tub bottoms (j) and 2 brown tub-tops (i). Cut batting and lining to fit tub bottom. Stack lining, tub bottom, and batting with right sides together. Sew around 2 sides and top. Turn. Stitch bottom of tub shut. Quilt around top and bottom edges and through center once. Quilt vertical lines for boards tub is made of. Sew tub tops together, right sides of fabric together, leaving opening for turning. Turn and stitch shut. Quilt around top edge and tack to each corner of lower part of tub at black dots. Tack tub to background in front of stove.

Step 8. Cut 2 light pink men (d). Interline with batting in the same manner as tub bottom. Turn right side out and quilt lines of arm, legs, and nose.

Embroidery and quilting guide, man

Embroider a solid stitch beard, hair, eyebrows, and eyes. Place man inside tub and tack. Tack a small piece of striped fabric in tub for washcloth.

Step 9. Sew white calendar (f) together and embroider date and *Sat.* on it. Attach double strand of thread at each upper corner. Tack string in center to wall behind stove. The calendar hangs freely.

Rise and Shine

Materials:

Fabric	Yardage
Lining	1 sq. yd.
Batting	1 sq. yd.
Bright blue	½
Green	⅔
Four different brown and rust prints (at	
least), brown, red, yellow, and gold	⅙ each
Yellow and white quilting thread	1 spool each
Elastic, ½″ wide	40″
Gold and red embroidery floss	1 skein each
Polyester fiber	
22″ quilt hoop	

Method:

Step 1. Make background. Cut a curved horizon on one edge of green fabric. Applique it over blue. Press and trim excess blue from seam. Cut a 36″ circle from the piece. Cut a 36″ circle of lining and a 30″ circle of quilt batting. Stack the three layers with batting in middle. Trim ¾″ from lining and sew background over lining to form a casing for elastic. Insert elastic and tack ends together.

Step 2. Place background in hoop and smooth fabric.

Step 3. Cut yellow sun (l) and applique to right-hand corner of horizon. With yellow quilting thread, quilt 12 rounds around sun, starting with lines ¼″ apart and expanding this distance to ¾″. Quilt a small cloud-shape in left sky with white thread. Following line of horizon, quilt green into rows 1½″ apart using yellow thread.

Step 4. Make post. Cut a 6″ square of brown and one brown post top (a). Fold square, right sides of fabric together, and sew along one side. Pin post top in and sew. Turn post right side out and lightly stuff with polyester fiber. Sew bottom shut and tack post to lower center of green. Position so bottom of post will be on back side of hoop — 5½″ from elastic edge.

Step 5. Cut rooster. Fold fabric right sides together when cutting pieces to produce 2 roosters mirroring each other. Include seam allowance. Cut 2 red wattles (b), 2 gold legs (c), 2 red combs (d), 2 brown and rust print wings (e), 2 yellow bills (f), 2 brown and rust print feathers (g), 2 print feathers (h), 2 print feathers (i), 2 print feathers (j), 2 print feathers (k), and 2 brown bodies (m).

Step 6. Assemble rooster. Applique tail feathers together, matching notches. Applique feather units to body along dotted lines of pattern. Applique the cone, wattle, wing, bill, and legs to body. After both sides of rooster are finished, place right sides of fabric together and sew around them, leaving an opening at breast for turning and stuffing. Add enough fiber to breast to give it a healthy bulge. Stuff a light layer of fiber in feathers near body, but do not push fill out to tips of feathers.

Step 7. Quilt along feather seams. Satinstitch a red eye and outline the wattle and comb with red floss and chainstitches. Outline feathers and wings in gold with chainstitches.

Step 8. Perch rooster on post and tack feet to center of post. Tack bird to background at back of head, middle of body, and top center feather. Tail feathers will curve forward gently, and if a ceiling fan is in motion, they will flutter quietly.

In the Clearing

Materials:

Fabric	Yardage
Batting	1 sq. yd.
Lining	1 sq. yd.
Bright green	2/3
Bright blue	1/3
Green flowered	1/4
Brown flowered	1/8
Dark green, brown, gold	1/6 each
Elastic, 1/2" wide	40"
Embroidery floss:	
Green, brown, red, black, gold,	
and white	1 skein each
Polyester fiber	
22" quilt hoop	

Method:

Step 1. Place (a) on fold line of green flowered fabric and cut 1 large mountain. Cut mountain for left of scene (b) and a right-hand mountain (d) from brown flowered print. Cut 2 green mountains (c). Applique mountains to blue background, centering largest one. Cut curved horizon on green fabric and applique it to the mountains. Trim excess seam in back. Cut a 36" circle from background, lining, and batting, and layer them with batting in center. Trim 3/4" from lining, fold background over lining, and hem to make casing for elastic. Insert elastic and tack ends together.

Step 2. Place background in hoop and smooth fabrics.

Step 3. Quilt around curves of mountains and along horizon. Quilt round mounds in the green, symbolic of bunchgrass.

Step 4. Make flowers. Cut 4 gold circles, 2" in diameter (g). Sew 2 together and turn right side out. Satinstitch a brown center and chainstitch petals

Embroidery guide, flowers

to outline them with gold embroidery thread. Make 2 more gold flowers, 1 1/2" in diameter, and two 1" in diameter (h). Tack flowers to green and embroider green stem and leaves using chainstitches.

Step 5. Make deer. Cut 2 brown heads, (f). Sew with right sides of fabric together, leaving opening between ears. Turn and stuff. Sew opening shut and embroider features on deer. Satinstitch eyes, nose, and tongue. Make 2.

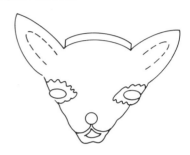

Embroidery and quilting guide, fawn head

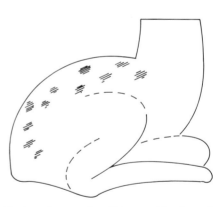

Embroidery and quilting guide, fawn body

Step 6. Cut 2 brown bodies (e). Sew right sides of fabric together, leaving the neck open. Turn and stuff. Stitch white spots on body and quilt lines of legs. Chainstitch hooves and tail. Make 2. Sew neck openings shut as they are sewn to backs of heads. Tack deer to background. Frame in a 22" hoop.

Sleeping Peasants

Materials:

Fabric	Yardage
Batting	1 sq. ft.
Lining	1 sq. ft.
Light green, gold, red, blue print, blue, pink, beige	⅙ each
Light blue	1 sq. ft.
Elastic, ¼″ wide	24″
Embroidery floss:	
Green, gold, red, black	1 skein each
White quilting thread	1 spool
Polyester fiber	
10″ quilt hoop	
(If 22″ hoop used, enlarge patterns three times.)	

Method:

Step 1. Make background. Stack lining, batting and light blue fabric together with batting in middle. Cut a 12″ circle. Trim ¾″ from lining, fold background fabric over lining, fold under ¼″, and sew to make casing for elastic. Insert elastic and tack ends together.

Step 2. Place background on hoop and smooth fabric. Cut light green grass (a and c) and applique to light blue.

Step 3. Cut gold strawstack (b) and applique to left side of grass. Cut red barn (d) and applique to upper right corner of grass.

Step 4. Make the man. Cut 2 pink bodies (f), sew with right sides of fabric together. Make a small slash in the back and turn right side out. Stuff very lightly with fiber and resew the slash. Cut 1 blue suit (j) and applique to figure. Turn outside edge seam

Quilting guide, suit

allowance to back of body. Quilt lines for head, collar, legs, and arm using white thread. Embroider hair and face. Cut 2 beige hats (e), sew, turn, stuff, and stitch to head. Embroider gold lines in hat.

Embroidery and quilting guide, man

Step 5. Make the woman. Cut 2 pink bodies (g), sew, turn, and stuff in same manner as man's body. Cut 1 blue print skirt (h) and 1 red blouse (i). Applique skirt first, then blouse to the top of the skirt.

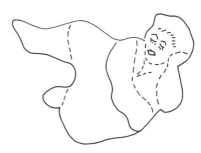

Embroidery and quilting guide, woman

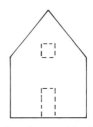

Embroidery guide, barn

Step 6. Attach the two figures with embroidery of woman's hair. Tack figures to background. Embroider green grass blades around green and gold stems in strawstack. Give barn a door and window. For more texture quilt around the patchwork until the entire circle is quilted. Make narror ¼″ rows of stitching.

Milk and Honey

Materials:

Fabric	Yardage
Lining	1 sq. yd.
Rust	1 sq. yd.
Gold and brown print (with rust, white, beige, and blue elements)	1/4
White	1/8
Brown	1/8
Gold	1/8
Brown satin ribbon, 1/2″ wide	3 1/2
White eyelet, 1 1/2″ wide	2
Batting	30″ square
Elastic, 1/2″ wide	40″
22″ quilt hoop	

Method:

1. Make background. Cut two 36″ circles, one from lining and one from background. Cut 30″ circle of quilt batting. Layer the three together and hem a casing for elastic. Insert elastic and tack ends together.

Step 2. Make Milk and Honey Bible block. Cut 4 print (a), 4 white (b), 4 print (c), 4 gold (d), 4 white (e), and 4 brown (f), folding fabric to reverse 2 pieces. Remember the 1/4″ seam allowances. Make block in quarters. Start with corner of each quarter section. Sew (a), (b), and (c) together. Sew (f) and (e) together. Join the two sections with (d). Make 4 and join.

Step 3. Add print borders. Cut two 14″ × 2 1/2″ strips and two 16″ × 2 1/2″ strips. Sew them to block. Press block and pin to center of rust background.

Step 4. Embroider quilting. Outline stitch gold pieces with gold floss, stitching through all thicknesses. Use white floss on white piecing and stitch down through center of brown with brown.

Step 5. Finish Bible block. Sew brown ribbon on seam line between block and print border and also around edge of print border. Using the hoop as a guide, mark circle on fabric. Sew eyelet 1/2″ from marked circle.

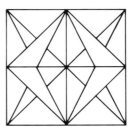

Milk and Honey Bible block

A Patchwork Miscellany

Carryall for Hoop-De-Do's

Like quilts, Hoop-De-Do's should not be stashed in plastic bags. It is unwise to fold scenes as some of the materials wrinkle, and if a quilted design is ironed, the result is a flat and lifeless picture. This bag is both storage and carryall. If you travel the craft and quilt show circuit, this is an ideal way to transport hoop and all — lightweight, not much larger than some purses, but big enough to accommodate a hoop and several scenes.

Materials:

Fabric	Yardage
Blue denim	2½
Print	½
Bright blue	¼
Pink	¼
Purple	¼
Yellow	¼
Red	¼
Dark blue	¼
Gold	3″ square
Batting	2½
Blue quilting thread	1 spool
Blue zippers, 12″	2

Method:

Step 1. Cut 2 denim and 1 batting circles 25″ in diameter. Cut 1 strip batting and 2 strips denim 3½″×53″, 2 strips denim 2½″×27″ and two 3″×12″.

Step 2. Make quilted inset. Install zippers between 2½″ strips of fabric. Zipper tabs meet in the center and open outward. Lay the 53″ denim and batting strips together and quilt with 2 rows of evenly spaced stitching. Sew this piece to the zippers to make a circle.

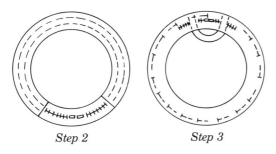

Step 2   *Step 3*

Step 3. Sew 12″×3″ strips into a double thickness, turning edges toward center to make handle. Pin

handle on denim bag back, right sides of fabric together, with handle ends 3″ apart. Pin the zipper inset to bag back, with one handle positioned in center of zippers.

Step 4. Make rainbow design for bag front. Cut 2 bright blue strips for curved center (a), 2 red (b), 2 yellow (c), 2 pink (d), 2 purple (e), and 2 dark blue (f), including ¼″ seam allowances. Sew together to form 2 quarter-sections. Cut 2 print quarter-sections. Sew 2 print and 2 patchwork sections together to make a circle. Press.

Step 5. Place 25″ circle batting on remaining denim circle and pin together with patchwork section. Quilt along the seams of the solid colors in the patchwork. Quilt three evenly spaced lines through the print sections (dotted lines). Applique 2½″ gold circle to center of design.

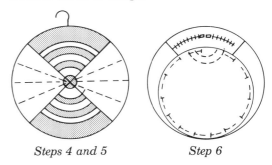

Steps 4 and 5   *Step 6*

Step 6. Pin a handle in center of solid color patchwork. Match front and back handles and pin front of bag to inset, right sides of fabric together. Sew around it *twice*.

Step 7. Turn bag through zipper opening. To store bag in closet, slip coat hanger under zipper.

Quilted Jacket

There are some machine quilted fabrics on the market but the advantage in quilting your own comes from the wide selection of fabric you could use. It is possible to quilt a jacket to match a skirt in prints, plains, or whatever. They can be dressy or casual according to the fabric. The teens love the small prints to wear with blue jeans (and so do I). For this project I chose a red, cotton-polyester blend with a white nub. It is a soft fabric that is easy to quilt, washable, durable, and goes well with slacks, jeans, or a skirt.

Method:

Step 1. Select a pattern with a minimum of seams; two side seams, two shoulder seams, one sleeve seam. A no collar pattern is best. Eliminate bulky cuffs and pockets. Buy a pattern one size larger than you usually wear to allow for quilting. Purchase required yardage of solid fabric, lightweight batting, and sheath lining.

Step 2. Launder fabric if you plan to wash finished jacket. Press fabric and cut batting and jacket fabric according to pattern directions. Cut lining ½″ larger than pattern. (You trim this later.)

Step 3. Pin layers together around edge of each pattern unit. Starting in center, baste outward on each unit to make four sections. Draw line with dressmaker's chalk down center of each piece. Quilt this line from top to bottom. Draw lines 1¼″ to right and left of center line and quilt from top to bottom. Do this until each piece is completely quilted. *Always* quilt in one direction and from the center out.

Step 4. After quilting is finished, assemble jacket according to pattern directions. If the jacket has a front lapel, leave it unquilted, but topstitch around its edge and around jacket bottom.

Matching Bag

Materials:

Fabric	Yardage
White fabric (for outside of bag)	½
Sheath lining (to match quilted jacket)	½
Batting	½
Bias tape, 1½″ wide (to match quilted jacket)	4
Jacket fabric to make flower and leaves	Scraps
Embroidery thread (to match quilted jacket)	1 skein
White quilting thread	1 spool

Method:

Step 1. Make bag front and back. Cut 18″ × 16″ rectangles from lining, batting, and white outer fabric. Pin lining, batting, and white together to make two bag sides. Lay these aside.

Step 2. Make flowers. Cut 2 flowers (a), 4 leaves (b), and 2 centers (c). With right sides of fabric together, sew around flower with ¼″ seams. Clip, cut slit 1″ long in center of one side of flower, and turn right side out. Stuff flower for a soft sculptured effect and stitch opening shut. With embroidery floss, chain-stitch to outline petals. Sew 2 flower centers together, slit one, and turn. Stitch opening shut and attach to flower with several French knots. Center flower on bag front and pin in place. Pin a leaf at each corner. Remove flower and applique leaves. Stitch flower to bag from underside, about 1″ from edge of petals. The soft flower will stand out from the bag.

Step 3. Quilting. Stitch around the leaves and petals

tack

Step 4

three times at ½″ intervals. Draw the quilting pattern on bag back. Quilt 3 rows, flower, and center.

Step 4. Trim bag front and back to 15″ × 17″. Round top and bottom. Trim batting to ½″ seam allowance in both front and back. Apply bias tape to both front and back. Place front and back of bag together with lining inside. Start sewing bag together 12″ from bottom edge. Stitch through all thicknesses ⅛″ from edge of bias. Tack at top.

Step 5. Make handles. Cut two 12″ × 2″ pieces of jacket fabric for handles. With right sides together, sew long edge and across one end. Turn and stuff solidly with batting. Stitch end shut and pin handles to centers of bag front and back, with handle ends 3″ apart. Sew securely into place.

Hotpads

Smile a Mile Melon

Materials:

Fabric	Yardage
Lining	13″ square
Green	13″ square
Batting	13″ square
Red	8″ square
Elastic, ½″ wide	12″
Corrugated cardboard	10″ circle
Black embroidery floss	1 skein
White quilting thread	1 spool

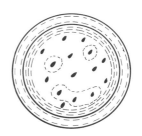

Embroidery and quilting guide, melon

Method:

Step 1. Cut circle 13″ in diameter from batting, lining, and green. Pin together. Trim ¾″ from lining and batting. Fold green to the back and stitch to lining to form casing for elastic.

Step 2. Cut red circle of fabric 8″ in diameter, and applique to green.

Step 3. With black floss, embroider sixteen melon seeds, using solid or satin stich.

Step 4. Quilt around the green melon rind twice. Each row is ¼″ apart. Make 3 rows of stitching into the red. Stitch around two seeds for eyes and around several seeds for mouth.

Step 5. Cut 10″ circle of cardboard. Run elastic through casing and slip hotpad over cardboard. Use under hot bowls to protect surfaces. When hotpad becomes soiled, remove cardboard, wash, dry, and replace cardboard for further use.

Egg Bert

Materials:

Fabric	Yardage
White lining	13″ square
Batting	13″ square
White (egg whites)	13 ″
Elastic, ½″ wide	12″
Gold fabric	5″ square
Corrugated cardboard	10″ circle
White quilting thread	1 spool
Navy, gold embroidery floss	1 skein each

Embroidery and quilting guide, egg

Method:

Step 1. Cut 13″ circle from batting, lining, and white. Pin together. Trim ¾″ from lining and batting. Fold white to back and stitch to lining to form casing for elastic.

Step 2. Cut gold circle 5″ in diameter and applique yolk to white, stuffing it slightly.

Step 3. Give yolk a happy face with navy satin-stitched eyes and a chainstitched mouth. Quilt with white quilting thread around yolk three times. Make a crisp fried edge with gold chain stitches.

Step 4. Cut 10″ circle of cardboard. Run elastic through casing and slip hotpad over cardboard.

Flirty Gerty Grapefruit

Materials:

Fabric	Yardage
Lining	13″ square
Batting	13″ square
Yellow fabric	13″ square
Elastic, ½″ wide	12″
Corrugated cardboard	10″ circle
White quilting thread	1 spool
Green, white embroidery floss	1 skein each

Method:

Step 1. Cut 13″ circles of batting, lining, and yellow fabric. Mark quilting lines in yellow fabric by pressing it into eight even sections.

Step 2. Pin the three layers together. Trim ¾″ from lining and batting. Fold yellow to the back and stitch to lining to make casing for elastic.

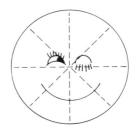

Embroidery and quilting guide, grapefruit

Step 3. Quilt along crease lines. Embroider eyes and mouth with green chainstitches. To make rind, chainstitch around edge with white.

Step 4. Cut 10″ circle of cardboard. Run elastic through casing and slip hotpad over cardboard.

Christmas Star Pillow

Materials:

Fabric	Yardage
White	½
Red	¼
Red candy cane print	¼
Green and white dotted	¼
Holly berry print	¼
Lining	½
Batting	½
White quilting thread	1 spool

Method:

Step 1. To make 16″ pillow, cut 56 diamonds (d), adding ¼″ seam allowance, as follows: 8 red, 16 red candy cane print, 16 green and white dotted, and 16 holly berry print. Cut 8 white background pieces (b).

Step 2. Assemble block in sections. Starting with star point (red diamond), add red print, green dot, then holly berry. Make 8 facing opposite directions.

Step 3. Sew 2 rows together for each star point. There are 4 complete points. Eliminating red diamond, make 8 more rows with 3 diamonds in each. Sew together, 2 rows for a point. These short points are sewn between the first 4 points assembled. Add white filler pieces (c). If you want a hexagonal pillow omit corners.

Step 4. Press as you go and trim seams. Lay seams over toward the print because seams show through white fabric.

Step 5. Cut 4 strips 13″ × 1¾″ of green dotted to fit each side of patchwork. Cut 4 red squares (e) for corners.

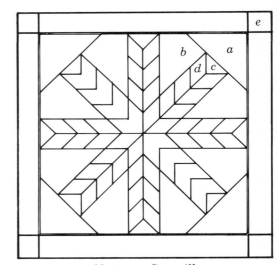

Christmas Star pillow

Step 6. On wrong side of block, spread out batting and trim within ¼″ from edge. Cut a 16½″ square of lining to cover batting.

Step 7. Pin layers together and, starting at center of star, outline quilt each pattern piece ⅛″ to ¼″ from seam.

Step 8. For envelope pillow back, cut two white pieces 16½″ × 20″. Make ¼″ hem on one 16½″ edge on each. Place the rectangles right sides of fabric together on pillow front. Overlap to form an envelope opening. Stitch in place making ¼″ seams. Double stitch on envelope overlap.

Christmas Stocking

This is a big stocking. It will hold a dozen oranges or two pounds of English walnuts or a number of trinkets.

Materials:

Fabric	Yardage
Blue washable velvet	½
Rose washable velvet	½
Rust washable velvet	½
Lining	½
Batting	½
Blue ribbon, ½″ wide	6″
Gold embroidery floss	1 skein

Method:

Step 1. To make a crazy patch stocking, sew together several small pieces of velvet until piece measures 16″ × 20″. Press and trim the seams.

Step 2. Using the pattern template, make freezer paper pattern. Fold patchwork together and cut two stockings, adding seam allowance. Sew back seam together.

Step 3. Do same with lining and batting. Pin three layers together and make herringbone stitches around each crazy patch. Stitch through all thicknesses. This serves as quilting. (For unquilted version exclude batting.)

Step 4. Pin stocking foot and front together, right sides of fabric together, and stitch with sewing machine. Turn top edge down and handstitch in place. To personalize stocking embroider name or initials somewhere on it.

Step 5. Tack ribbon to stocking back for hanging.

Bean Bags

Tropical Fish

Materials:

Fabric	Yardage
Patchwork	8″ × 12″
Polyester ribbon, ½″ wide	9″
Gold embroidery floss	1 skein
Beans	1 cup

Method:

Step 1. Construct 8″ × 12″ patchwork piece, using any fabric you have on hand. Press.

Step 2. Cut two fish bodies (a), including ¼″ seam allowance. Cut three 3″ strips of ribbon.

Step 3. Pin bodies, right sides of fabric together, with ribbons pinned to inside along notched edge. Sew, leaving opening for turning. Turn, fill with beans, and close opening.

Step 4. Embroider cross-stitch mouth and gold satin stitch eyes. Add embroidered detail as you wish—chainstitch stripes or dot with French knots. (See photograph in color section.)

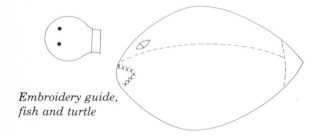

Embroidery guide, fish and turtle

Paintbox Turtle

Materials:

Fabric	Yardage
Patchwork	8″ × 12″
Polyester ribbon, ½″ wide	3″
Green embroidery floss	1 skein
Beans	1 cup

Method:

Step 1. Construct 8″ × 12″ patchwork piece, using any fabric you have on hand. Press.

Step 2. Cut two turtle bodies (a) and two heads (b), including ¼″ seam allowance.

Step 3. Pin head pieces, right sides of fabric together. Sew, leaving notched edge open. Turn. Embroider green satin stitch eyes.

Step 4. Pin head to notched edge of body pieces, right sides of fabric together. Sew. Pin body pieces, right sides of fabric together, with ribbon folded end to end and turned to the inside at tail. Sew, leaving opening for turning. Turn, fill with beans, and close opening.

Step 5. Embroider green satinstitch eyes. Add details as you wish—chainstitch with green floss to outline body and squares on shell or outline with white ribbon or gold cross-stitches. (See photograph in color section.)

Biter, Biter, Six-legged Spider

Materials:

Fabric	Yardage
Black	⅙
Yellow	⅙
Black yarn	2 oz.
Buttons	2
Beans	1 cup

Method:

Step 1. Cut one black body (a). Cut 4 black body sections (b) and 4 yellow body sections, including ¼″ seam allowance.

Step 2. Sew black and yellow sections together, alternating colors to make second 6″ circular body piece. Press.

Step 3. Lay three 10″ strands yarn on right side of pieced circle along six seam lines. Baste in place.

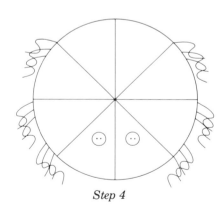

Step 4

Pin bodies, right sides of fabric together, with yarn inside. Sew, leaving opening for turning. Turn, fill with beans, and close opening.

Step 4. Braid six yarn-strand legs. Sew on button eyes.

A Footnote from Mary Jane

I began writing professionally in 1976. After attending a creative writing course given by Lynn Hall, an Iowa author of children's books, I was motivated into action. "Write about what you know," the class was told, and since I knew needlework, I began to write about needlework. I became a regular contributor to *Quilt World* magazine and have written for over a dozen other papers and magazines in addition.

Sewing has been a part of my life for as long as I can remember. At a very young age, my first efforts were devoted to the construction of tiny doll clothes and miniature quilts. After many years spent making quilts, placemats, and the like from other people's patterns, I developed a strong urge to experiment with my own designs.

It was fun, but never easy. I could never sit down and draw a pattern on paper exactly as it would be from start to finish. The originality and self-expression had to evolve as the project progressed. Only with persistence and patience was I able to create something truly my own.

Patchwork Plus! is my first book and is a presentation of original designs that are fun to do and (if you can bear to part with them) a pleasure to give as gifts. You'll find a lot of latitude for self-expression in these projects but, hopefully, I've removed the biggest hurdle for you: "Step One — hair pulling and pencil breaking."

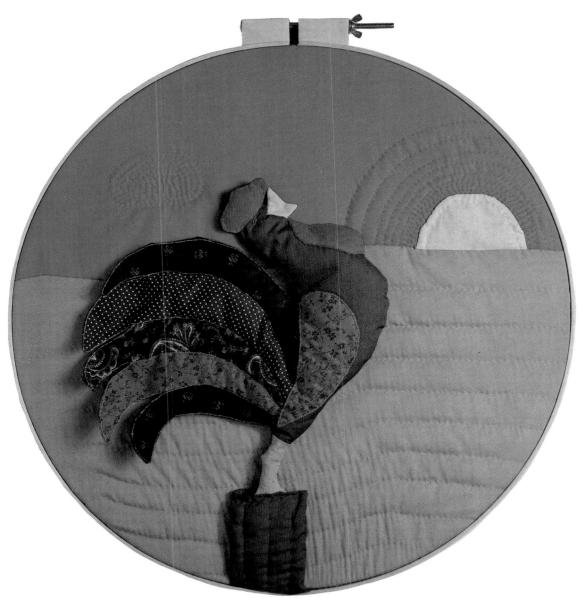

Rise and Shine

In the Clearing

Sleeping Peasants

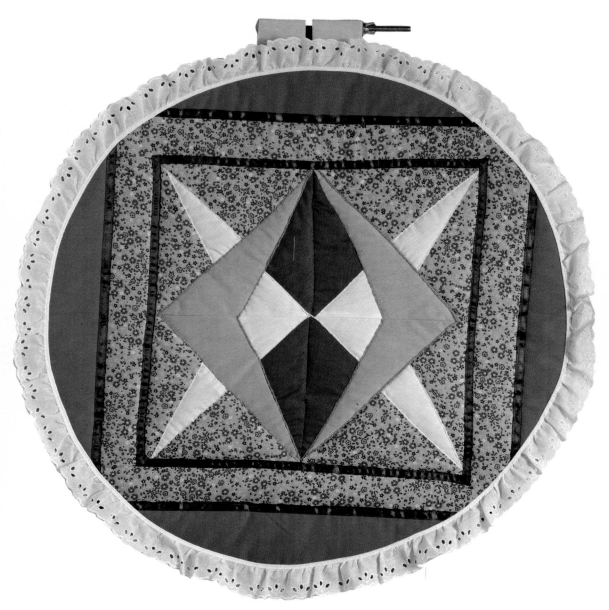

Milk and Honey

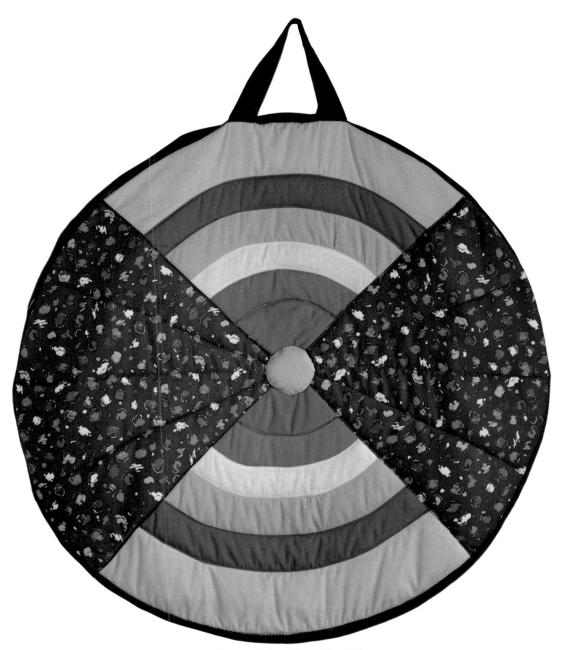

Carryall for Hoop-De-Do's

Quilted Jacket and Bag

Hotpads: Flirty Gerty Grapefruit, Smile a Mile Melon, Egg Bert

Christmas Star Pillow

Christmas Stockings

Tropical Fish, Paintbox Turtle Bean Bags

Spider Bean Bag

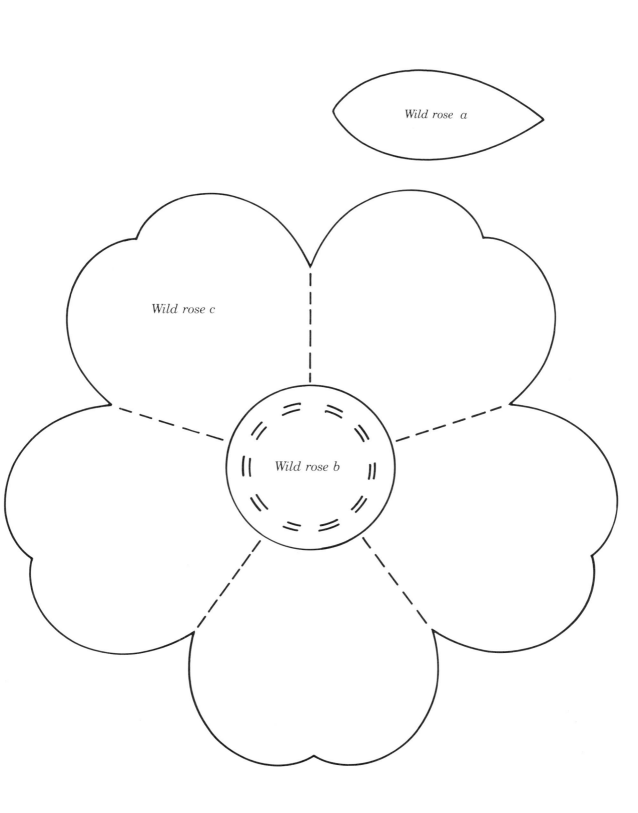

Wild rose a

Wild rose c

Wild rose b

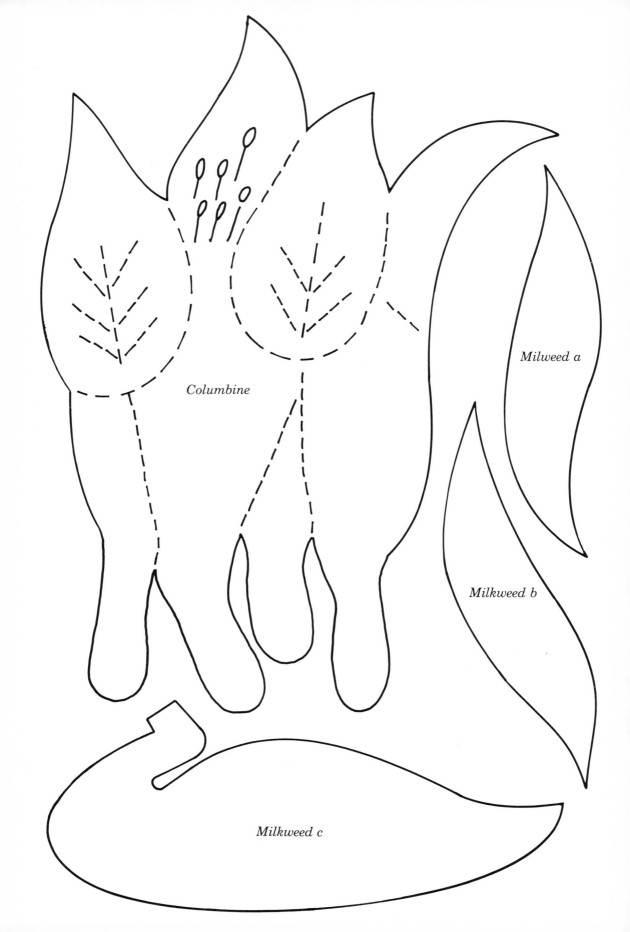

Milweed a

Columbine

Milkweed b

Milkweed c

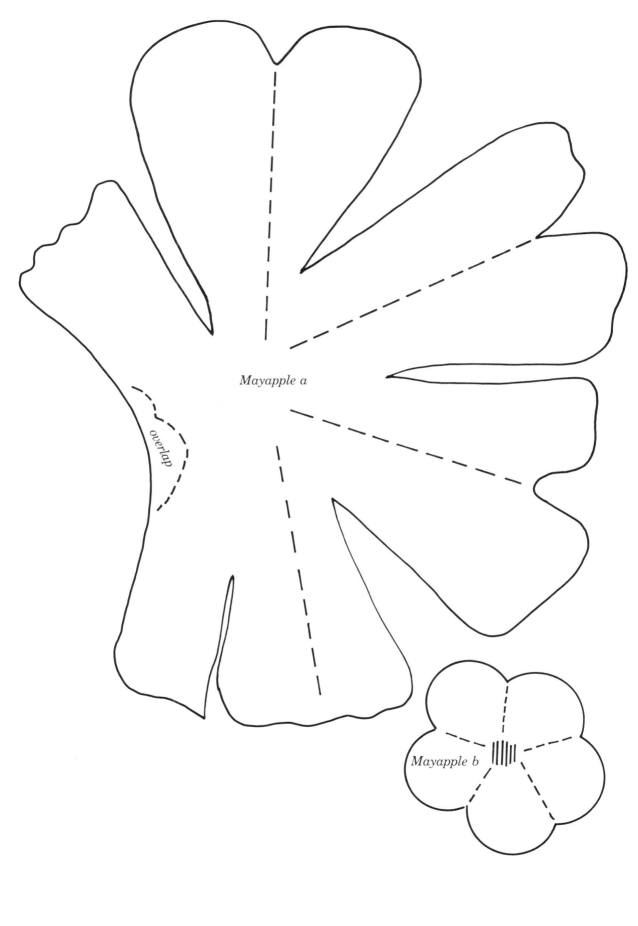

Mayapple a

overlap

Mayapple b

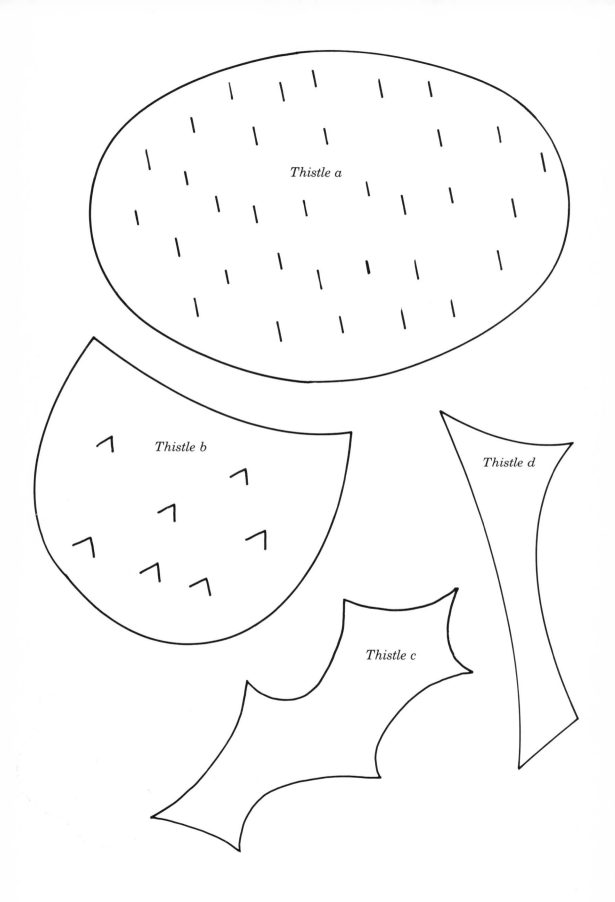

Thistle a

Thistle b

Thistle d

Thistle c

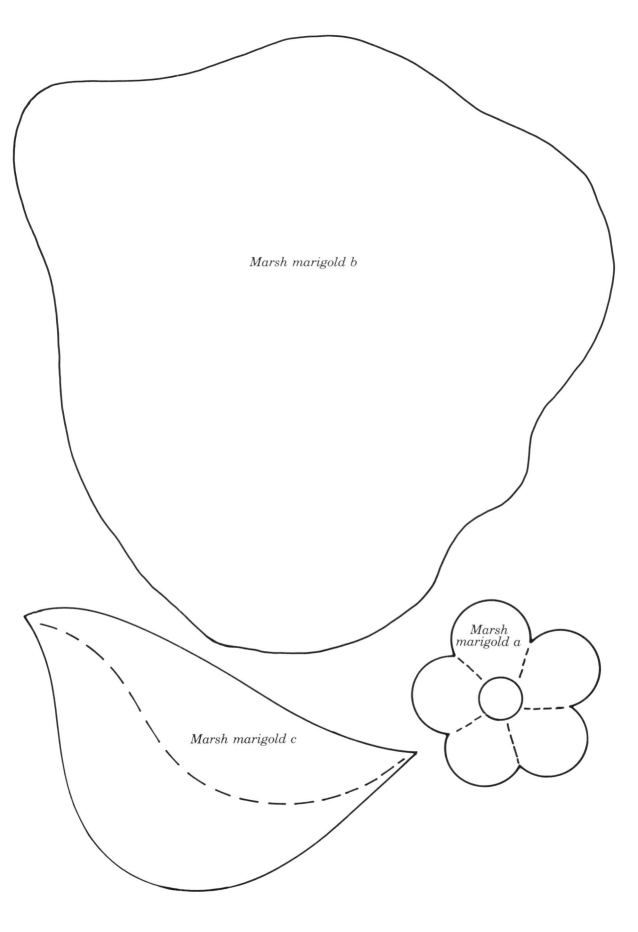

Marsh marigold b

Marsh marigold c

Marsh marigold a

Wild ginger b

Wild ginger c

Wild ginger a

Violet a

Violet b

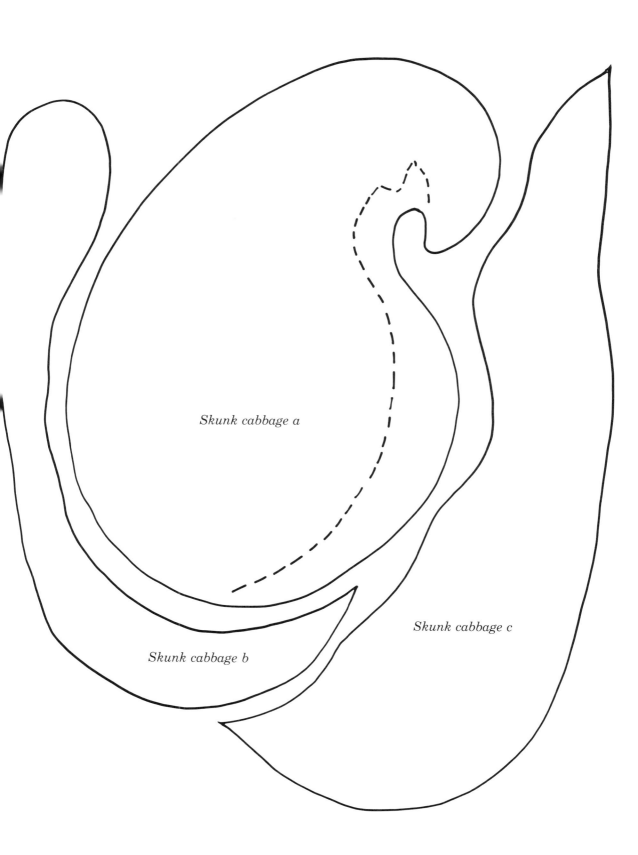

Skunk cabbage a

Skunk cabbage b

Skunk cabbage c

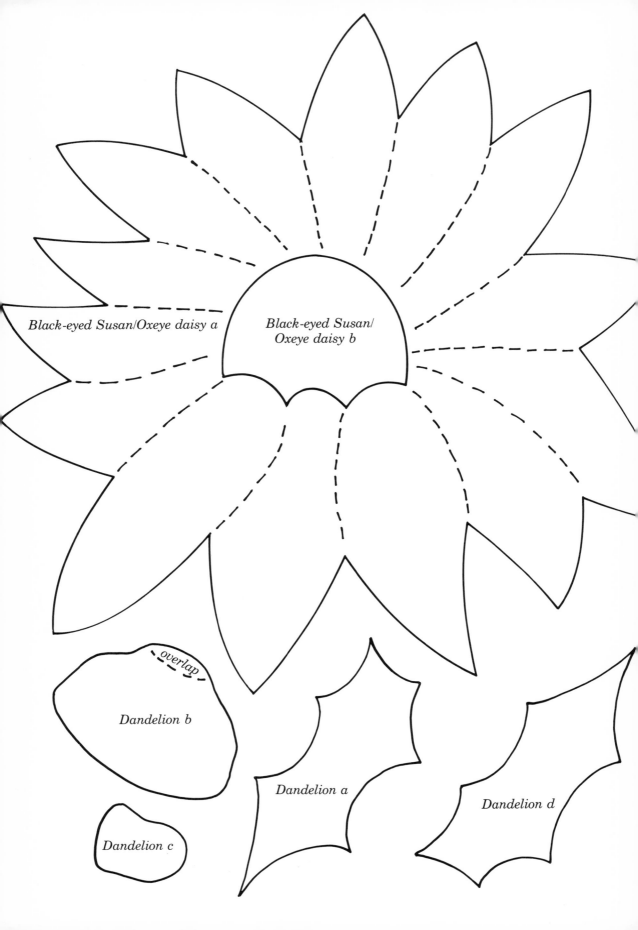

Black-eyed Susan/Oxeye daisy a

Black-eyed Susan/
Oxeye daisy b

overlap

Dandelion b

Dandelion a

Dandelion c

Dandelion d

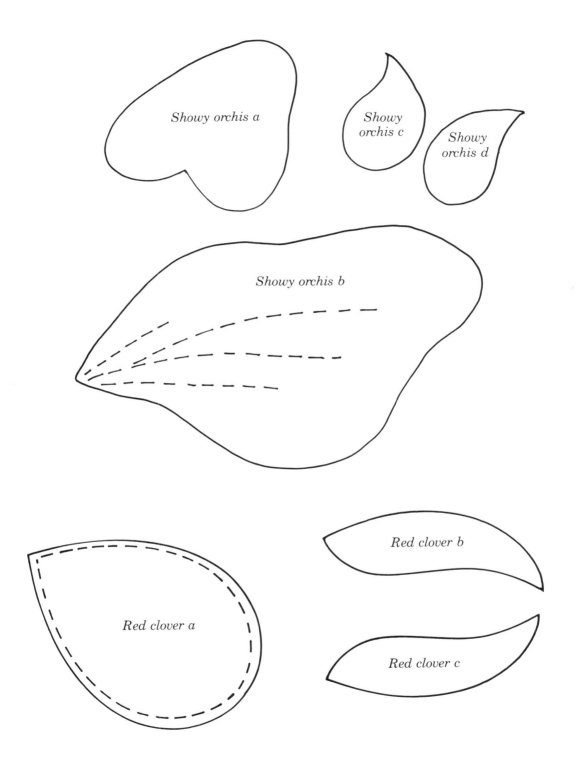

Showy orchis a

Showy orchis c

Showy orchis d

Showy orchis b

Red clover a

Red clover b

Red clover c

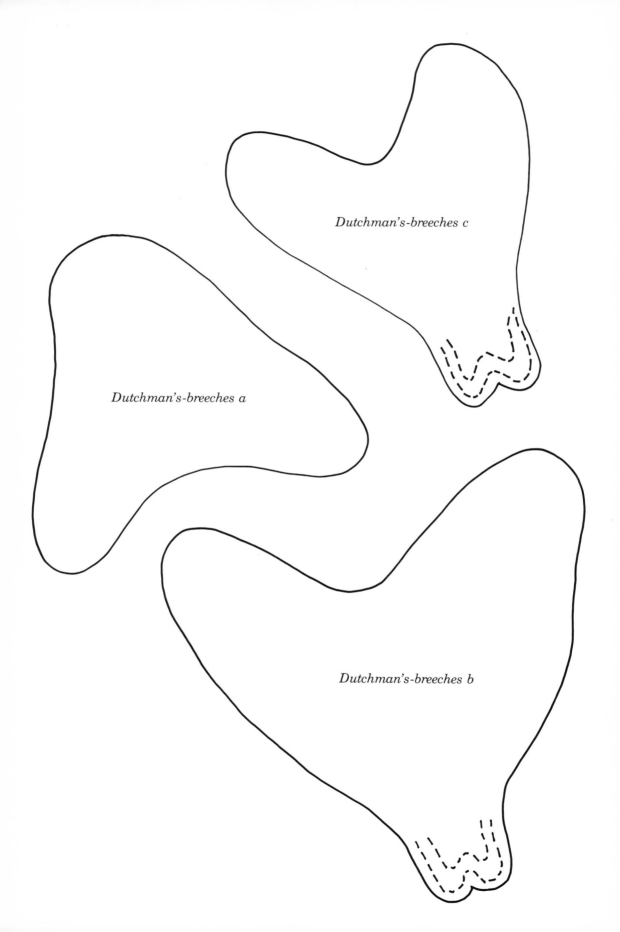

Dutchman's-breeches c

Dutchman's-breeches a

Dutchman's-breeches b

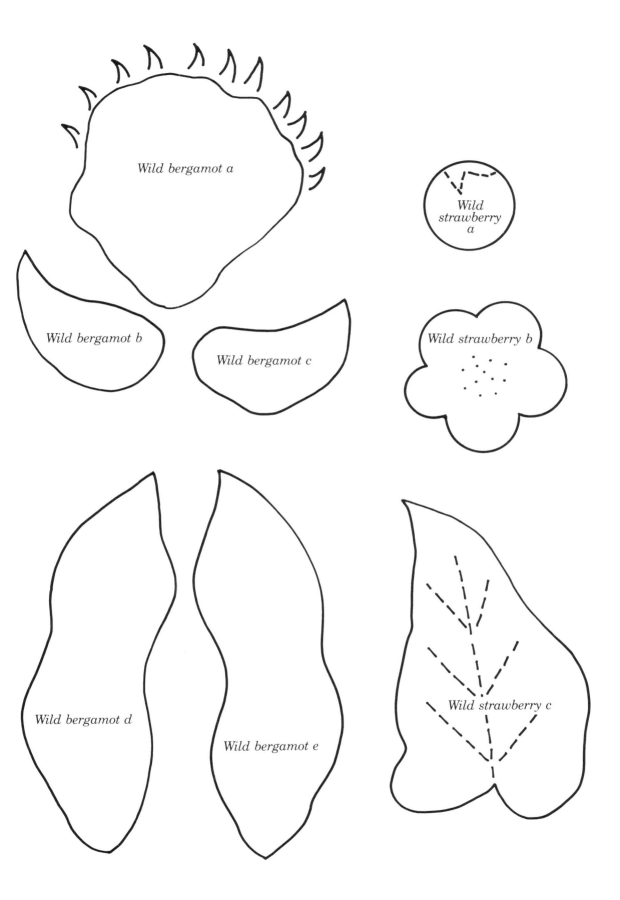

Wild bergamot a

Wild bergamot b

Wild bergamot c

Wild strawberry a

Wild strawberry b

Wild bergamot d

Wild bergamot e

Wild strawberry c

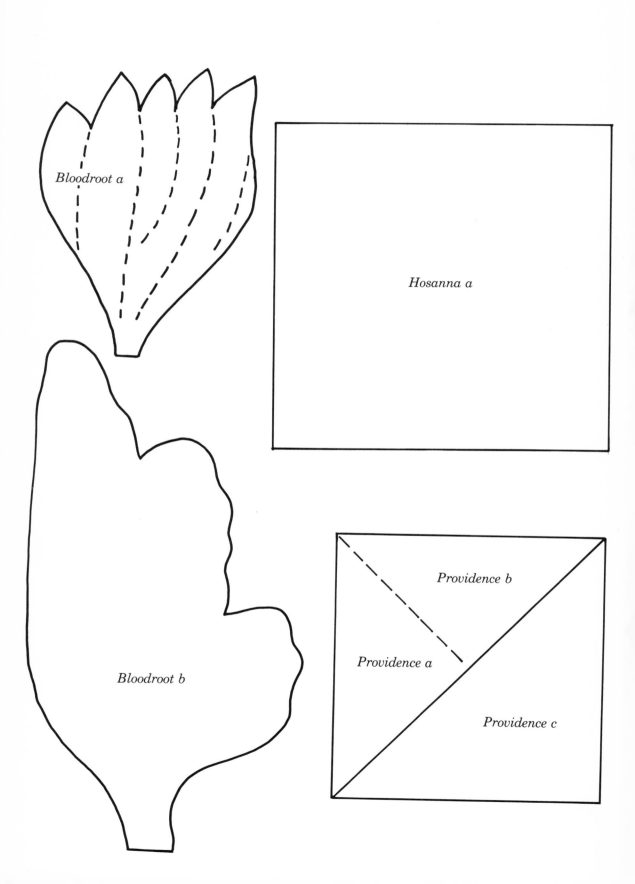

Bloodroot a

Hosanna a

Bloodroot b

Providence b

Providence a

Providence c

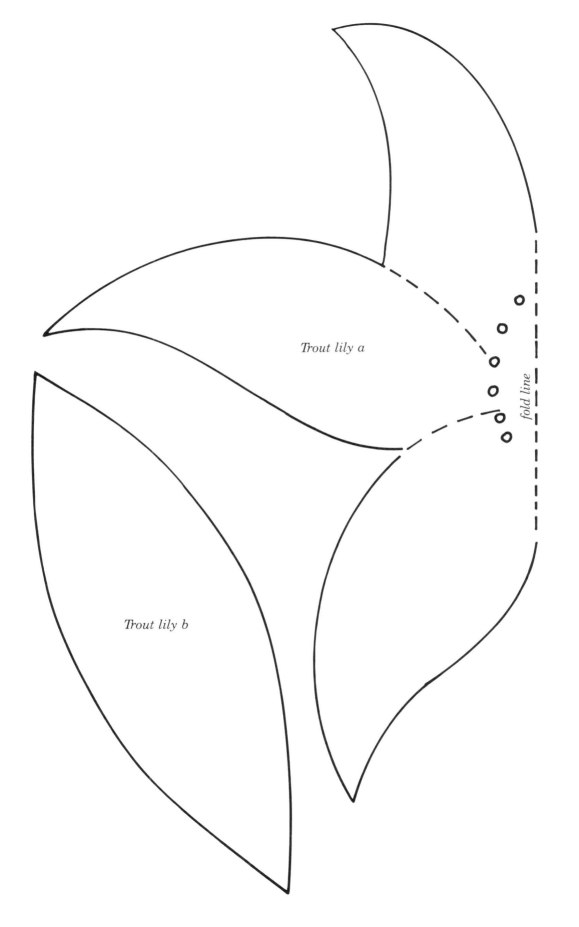

Trout lily a

Trout lily b

fold line

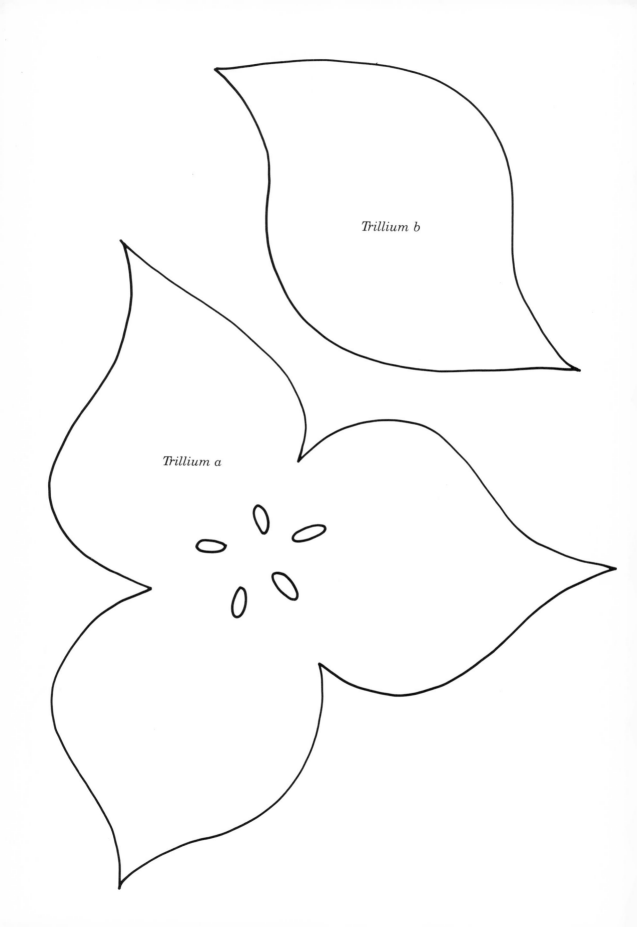

Trillium b

Trillium a

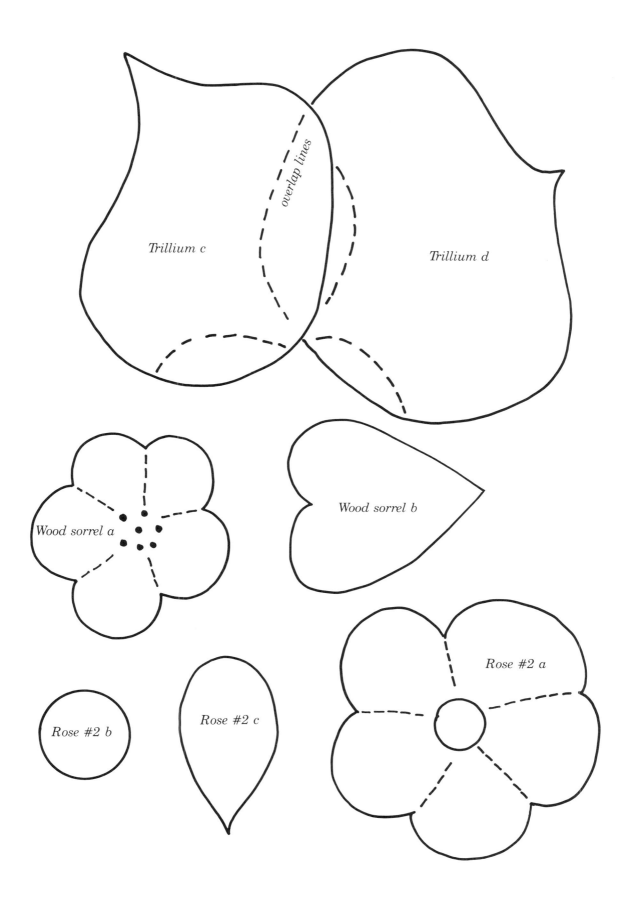

Trillium c

overlap lines

Trillium d

Wood sorrel a

Wood sorrel b

Rose #2 a

Rose #2 b

Rose #2 c

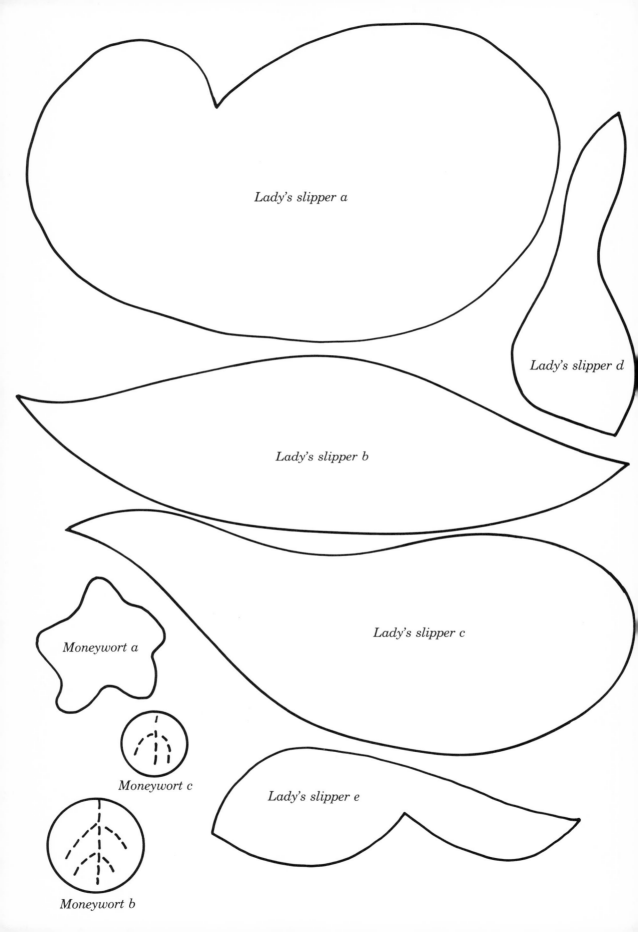

Lady's slipper a

Lady's slipper d

Lady's slipper b

Lady's slipper c

Moneywort a

Moneywort c

Lady's slipper e

Moneywort b

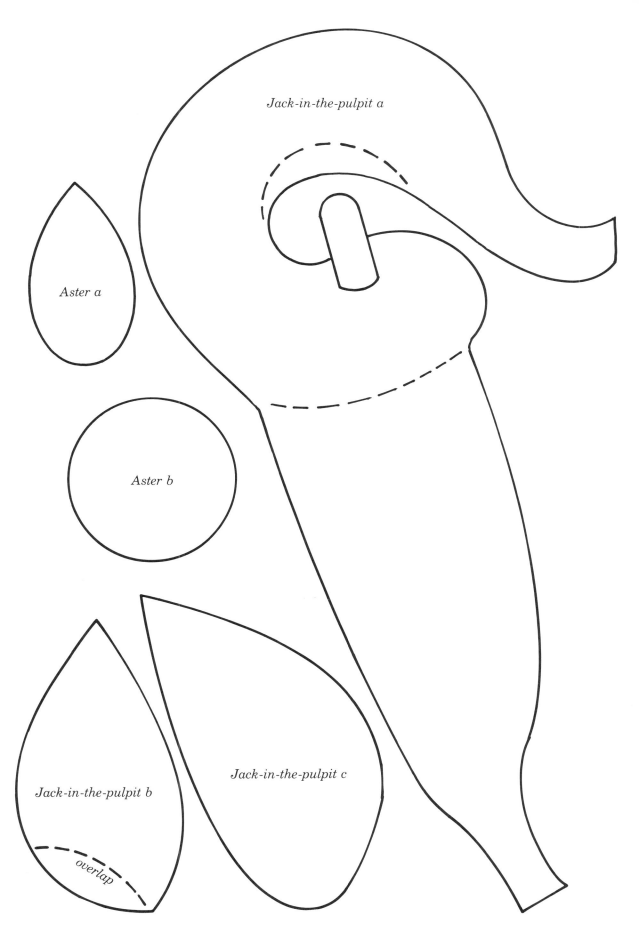

Jack-in-the-pulpit a

Aster a

Aster b

Jack-in-the-pulpit b

overlap

Jack-in-the-pulpit c

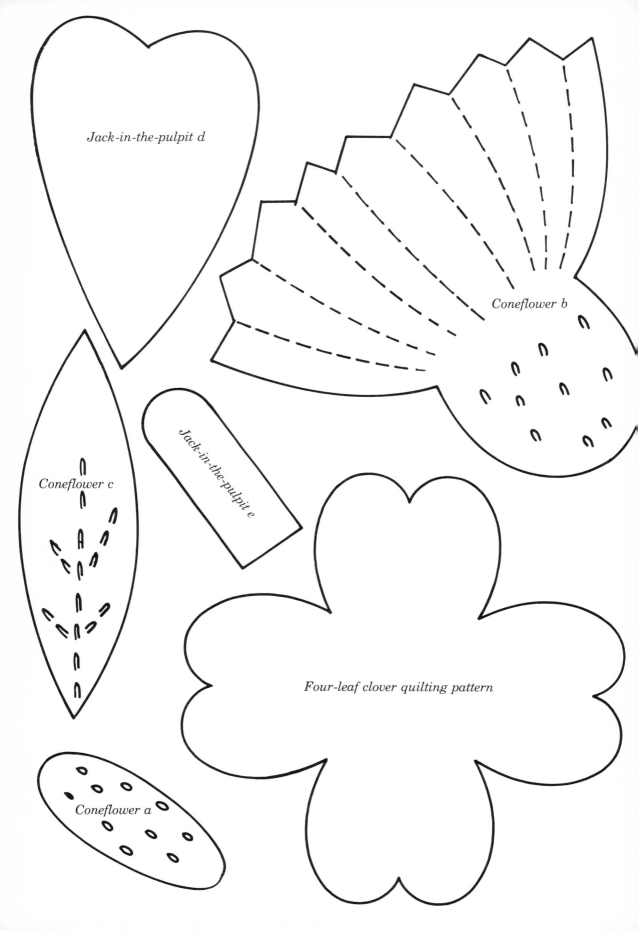

Jack-in-the-pulpit d

Coneflower b

Coneflower c

Jack-in-the-pulpit e

Four-leaf clover quilting pattern

Coneflower a

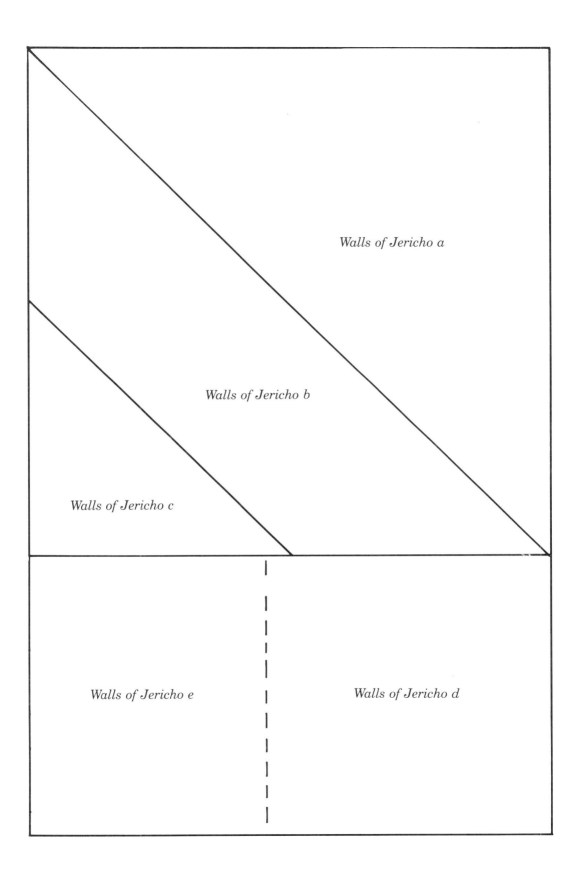

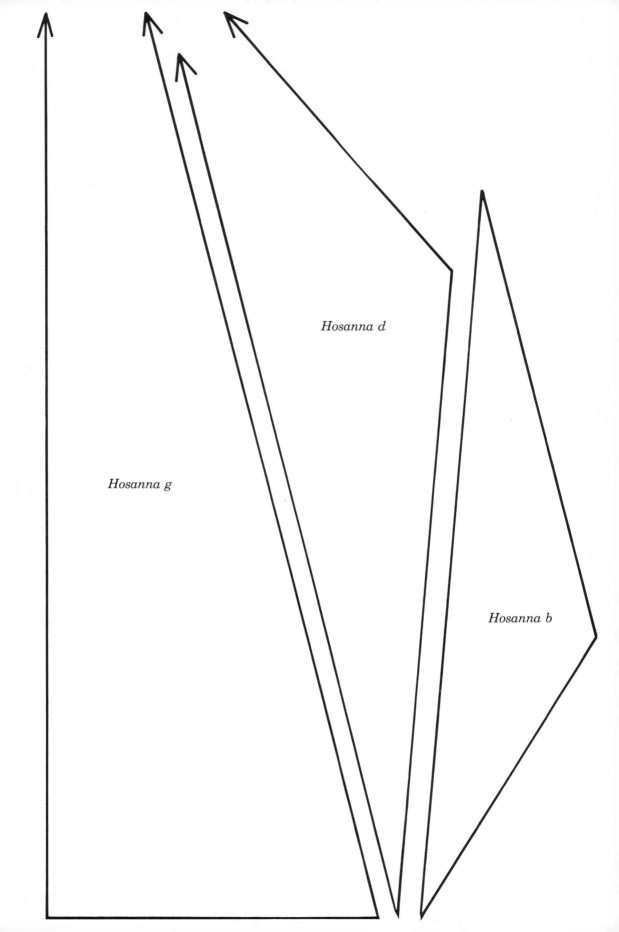

Hosanna d

Hosanna g

Hosanna b

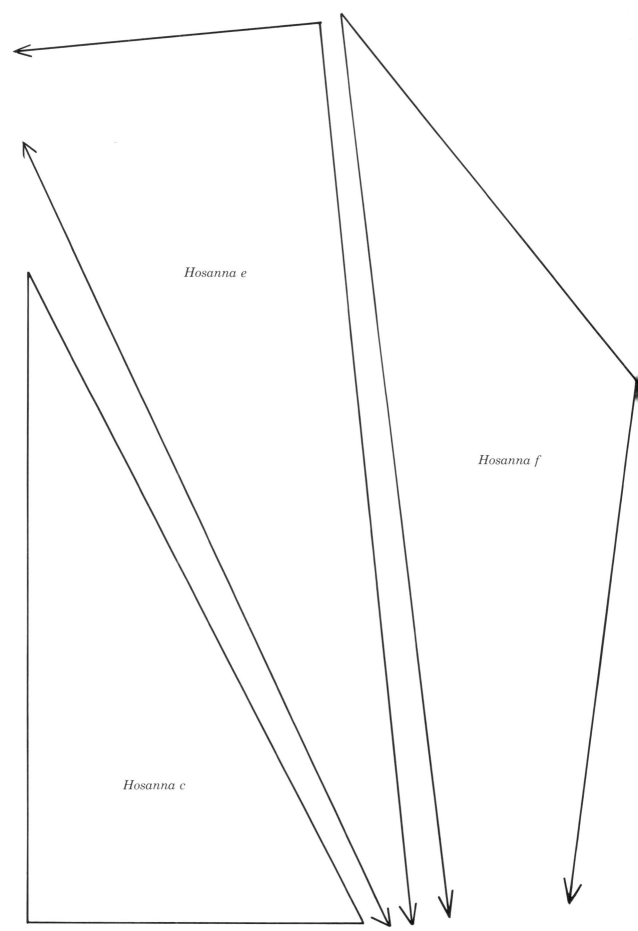

Hosanna e

Hosanna f

Hosanna c

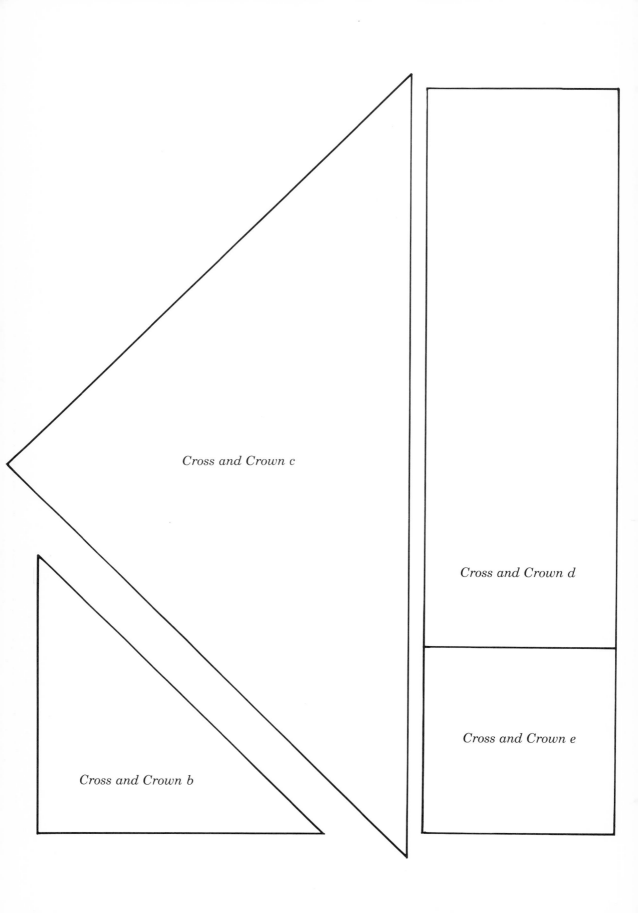

Cross and Crown c

Cross and Crown d

Cross and Crown e

Cross and Crown b

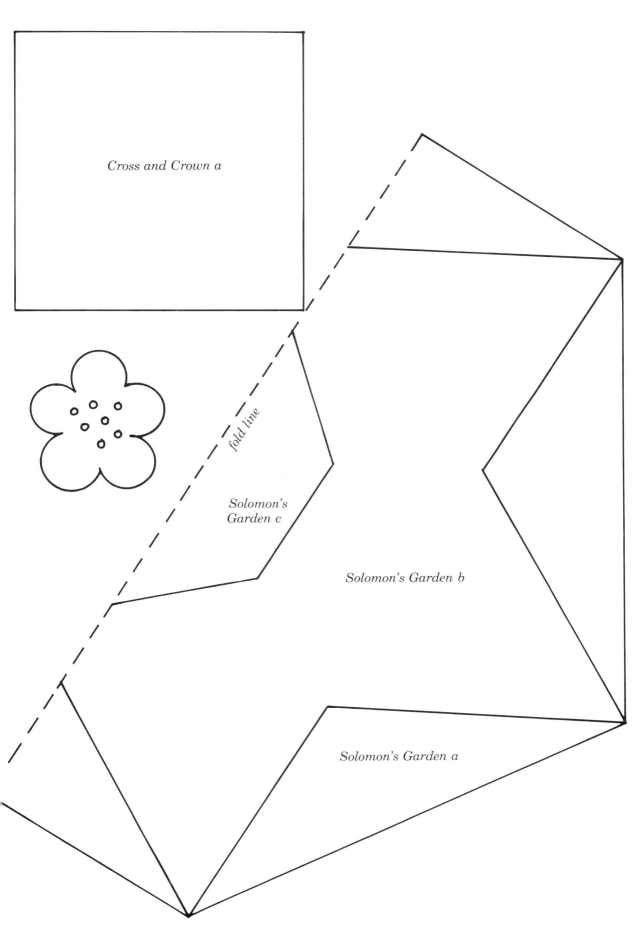

Cross and Crown a

fold line

Solomon's
Garden c

Solomon's Garden b

Solomon's Garden a

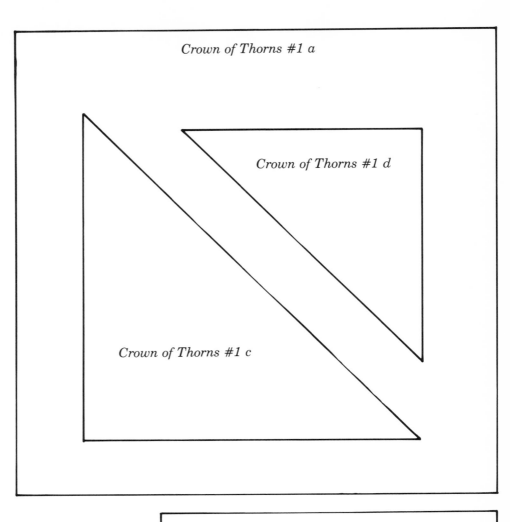

Crown of Thorns #1 a

Crown of Thorns #1 d

Crown of Thorns #1 c

Crown of Thorns #1 b

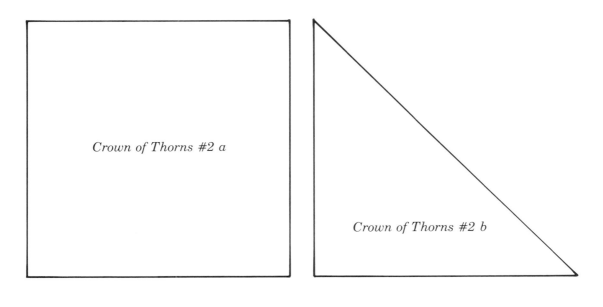

Crown of Thorns #2 a

Crown of Thorns #2 b

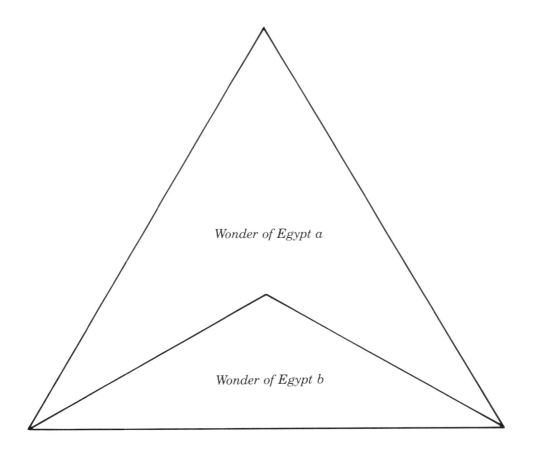

Wonder of Egypt a

Wonder of Egypt b

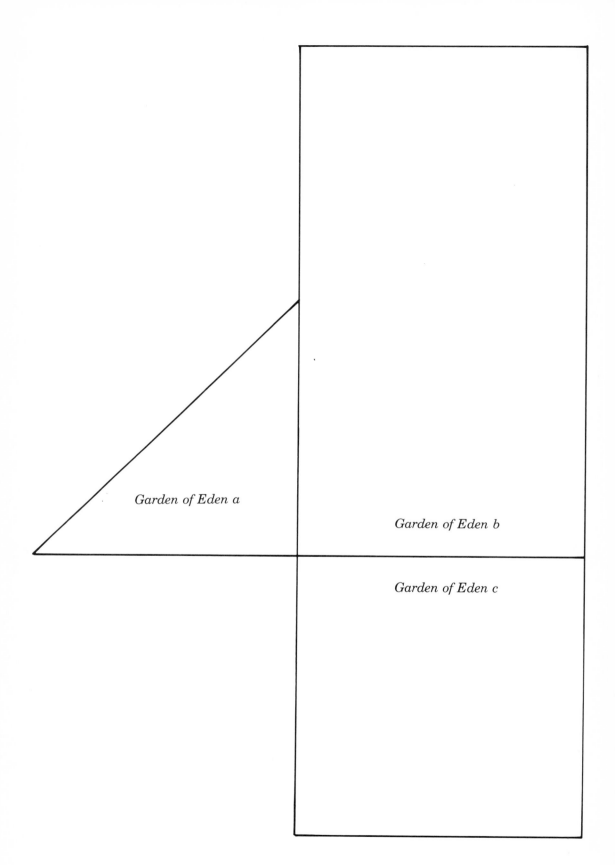

Garden of Eden a

Garden of Eden b

Garden of Eden c

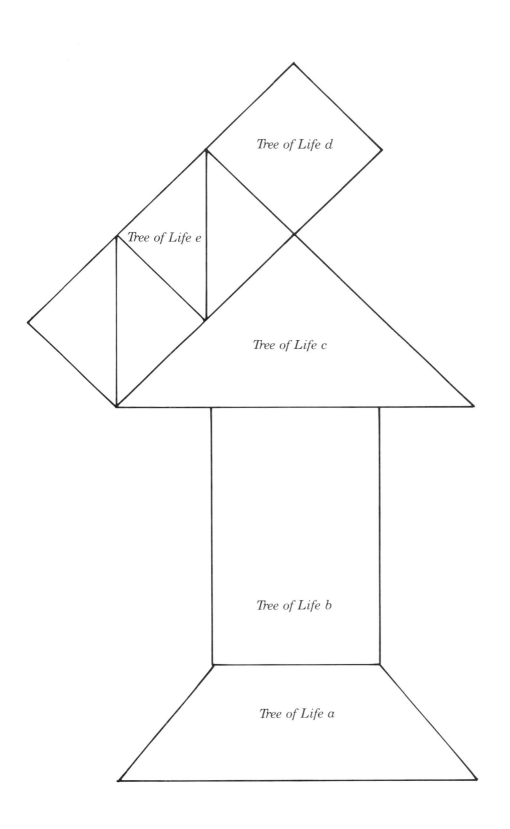

Tree of Life d

Tree of Life e

Tree of Life c

Tree of Life b

Tree of Life a

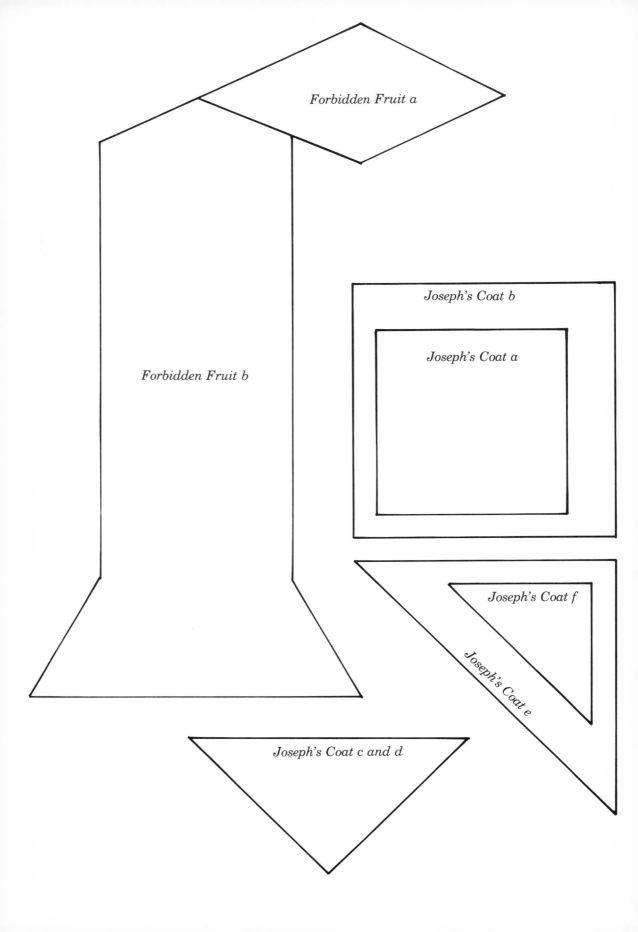

Forbidden Fruit a

Forbidden Fruit b

Joseph's Coat b

Joseph's Coat a

Joseph's Coat f

Joseph's Coat e

Joseph's Coat c and d

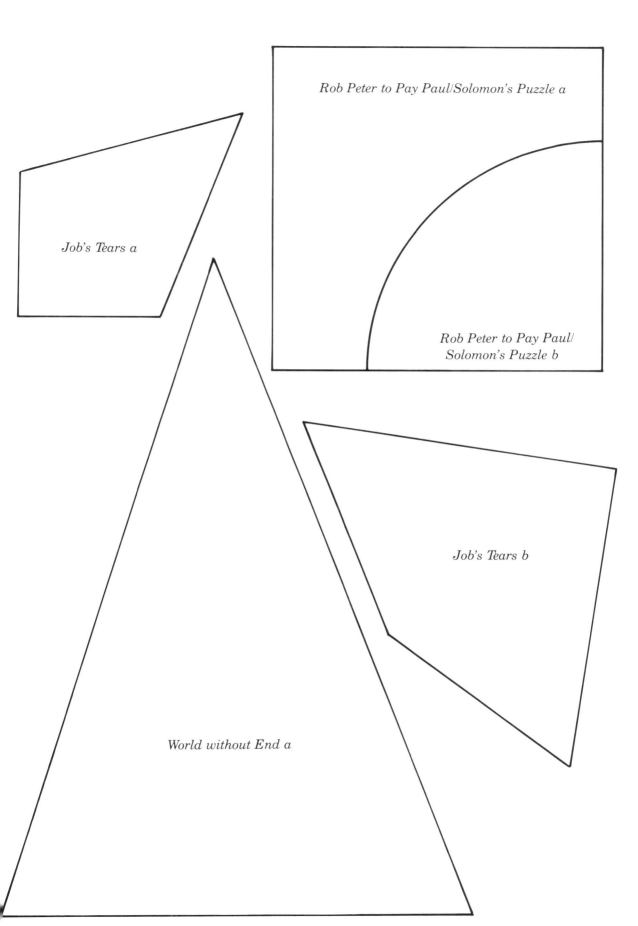

Job's Tears a

Rob Peter to Pay Paul/Solomon's Puzzle a

Rob Peter to Pay Paul/
Solomon's Puzzle b

Job's Tears b

World without End a

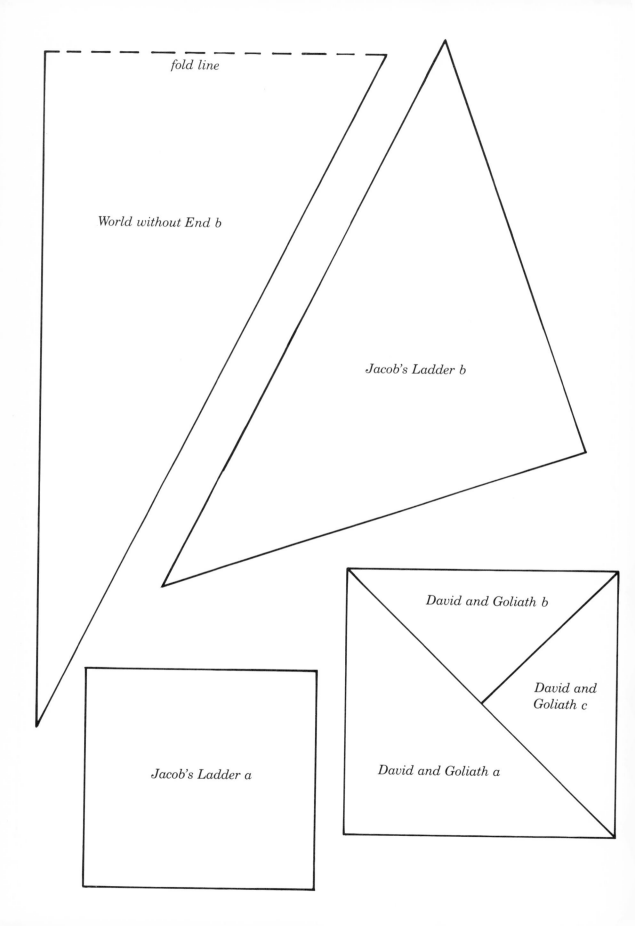

fold line

World without End b

Jacob's Ladder b

David and Goliath b

David and Goliath c

Jacob's Ladder a

David and Goliath a

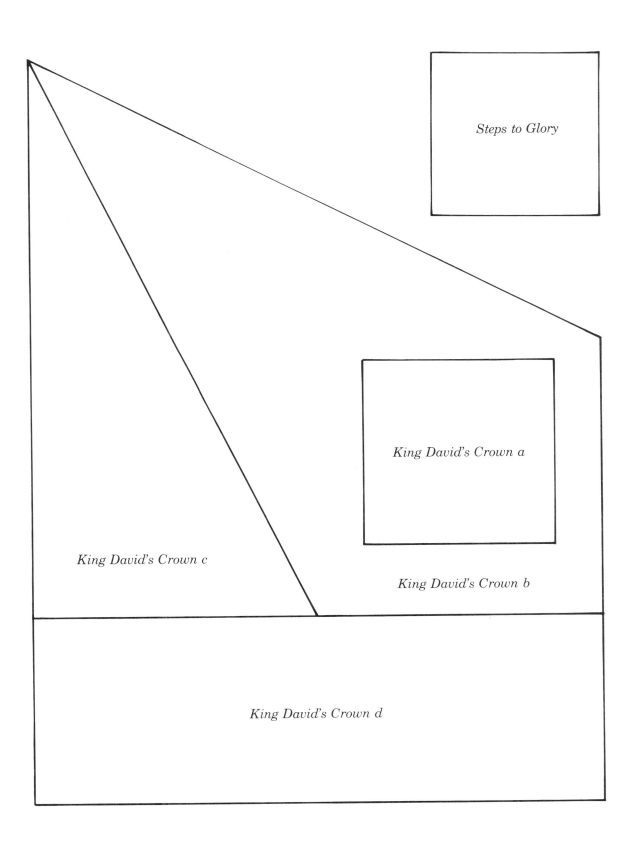

Steps to Glory

King David's Crown a

King David's Crown c

King David's Crown b

King David's Crown d

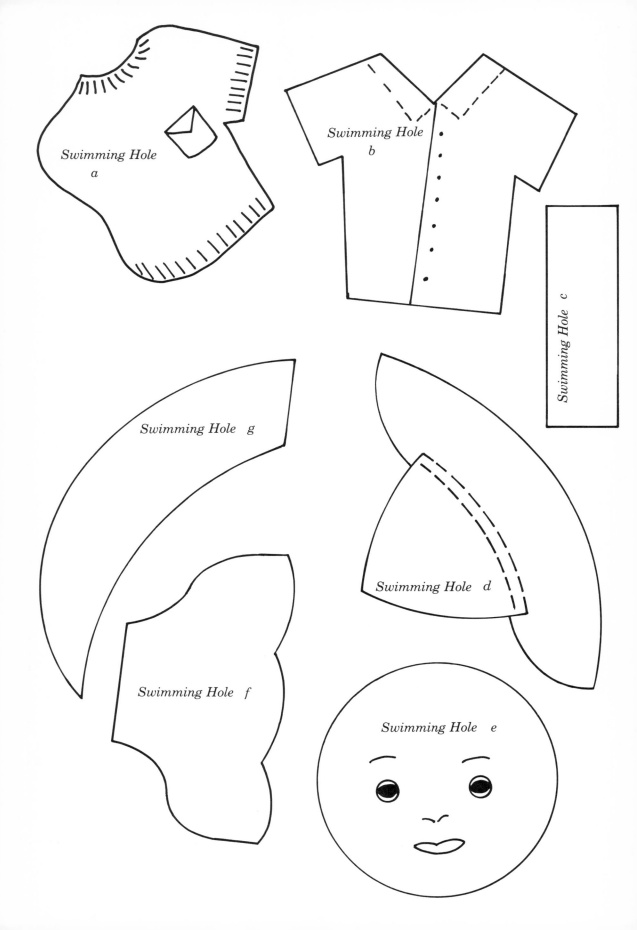

Swimming Hole
a

Swimming Hole
b

Swimming Hole c

Swimming Hole g

Swimming Hole d

Swimming Hole f

Swimming Hole e

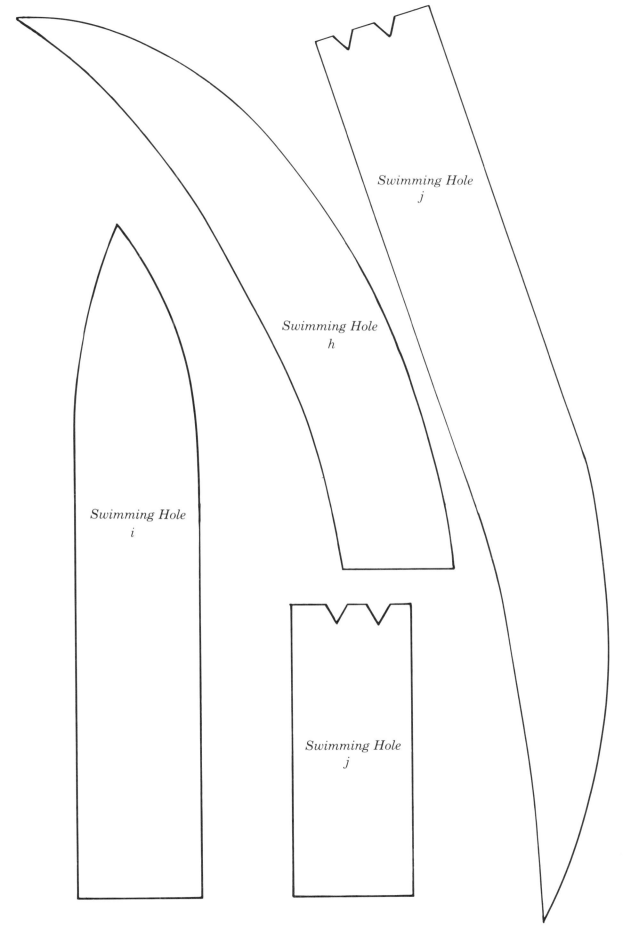

Swimming Hole
j

Swimming Hole
h

Swimming Hole
i

Swimming Hole
j

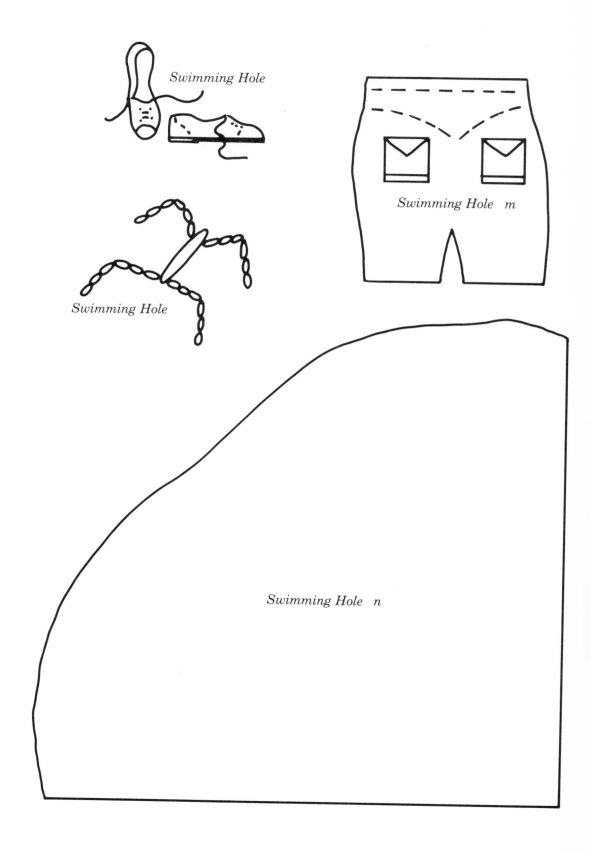

Swimming Hole

Swimming Hole m

Swimming Hole

Swimming Hole n

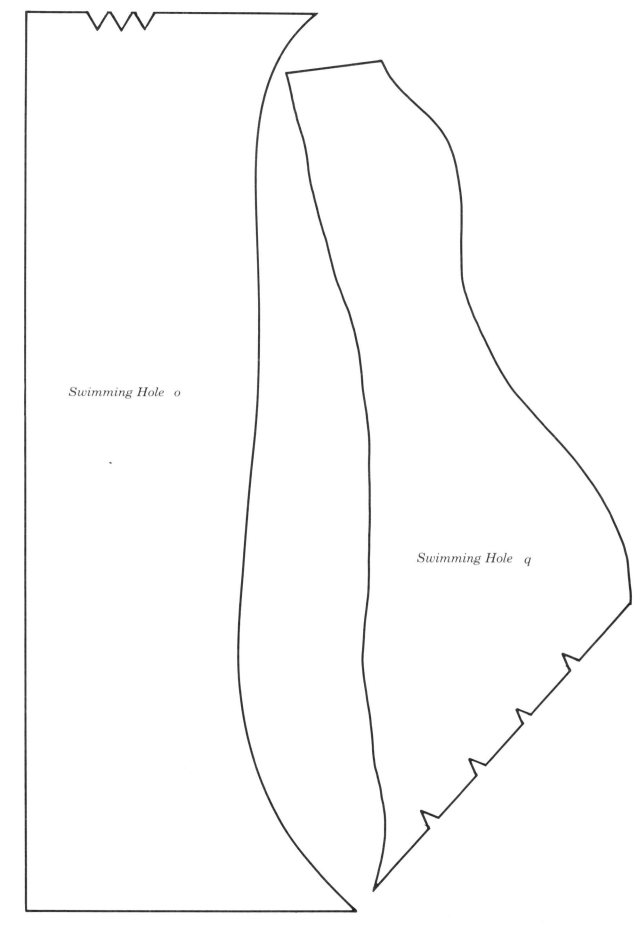

Swimming Hole o

Swimming Hole q

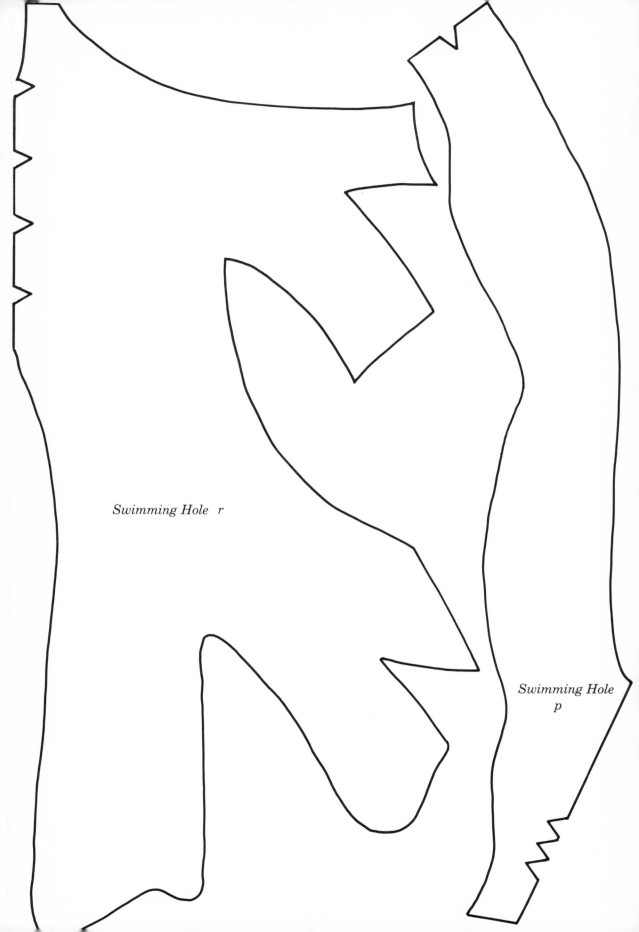

Swimming Hole r

*Swimming Hole
p*

Swimming Hole t

Swimming Hole s

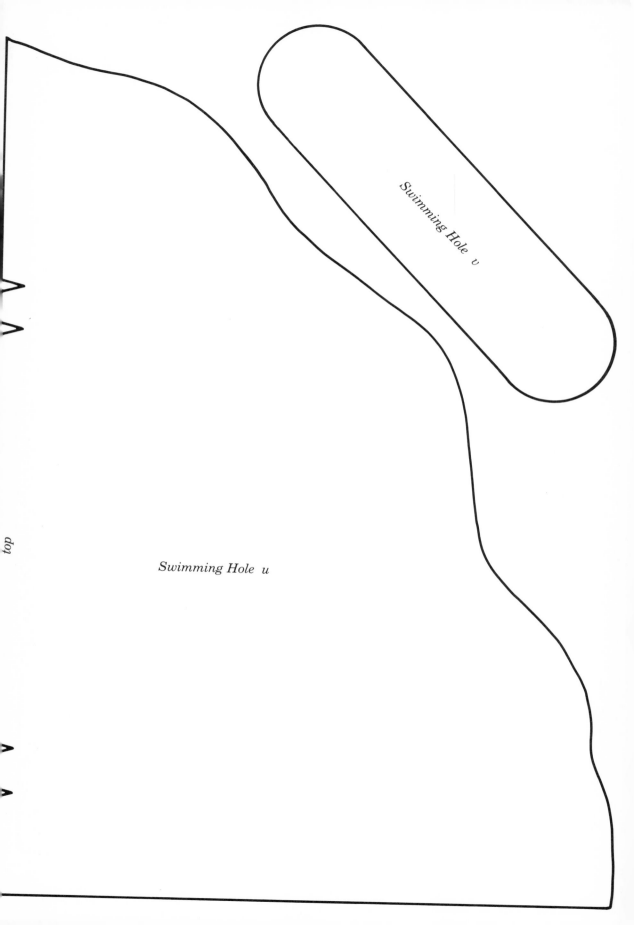

Swimming Hole *v*

Swimming Hole *u*

top

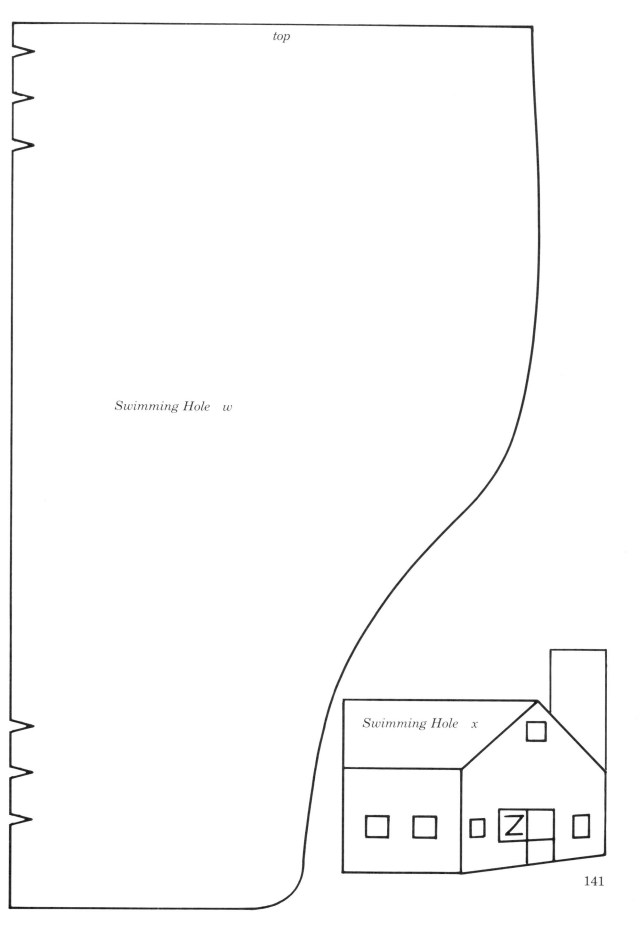

top

Swimming Hole   w

Swimming Hole   x

Z

141

Swimming Hole
aa

Swimming Hole   y

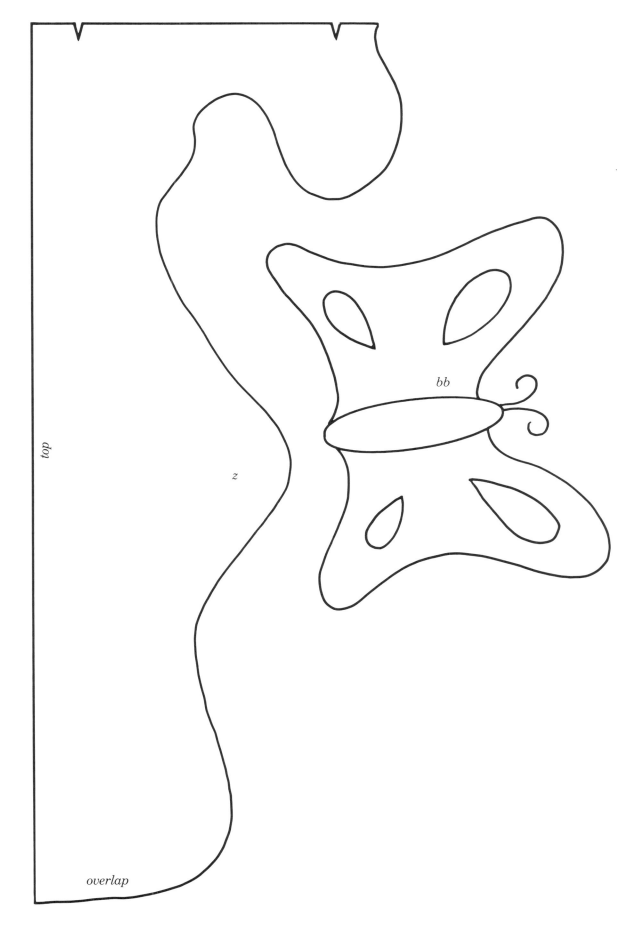

top

z

bb

overlap

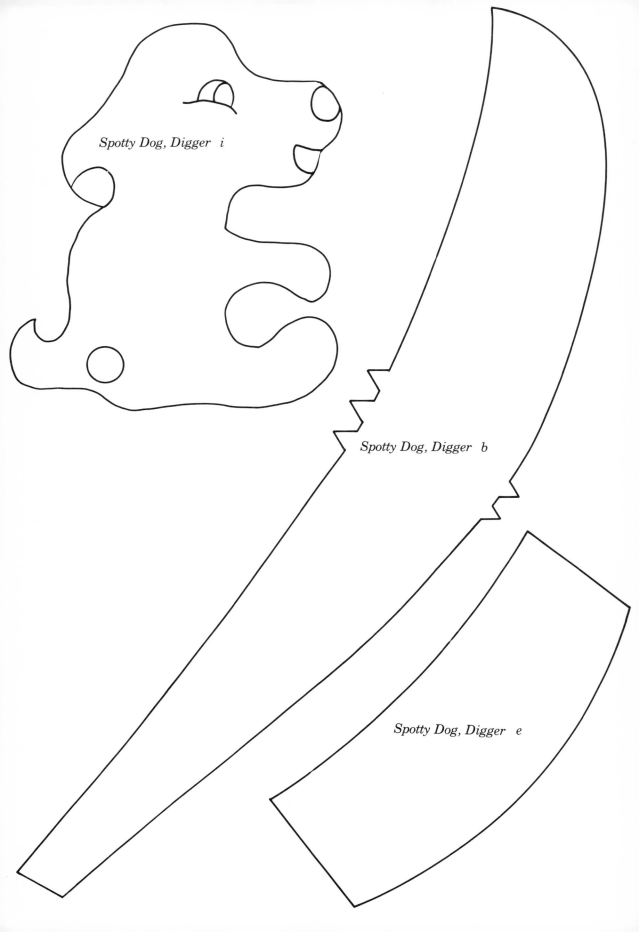

Spotty Dog, Digger i

Spotty Dog, Digger b

Spotty Dog, Digger e

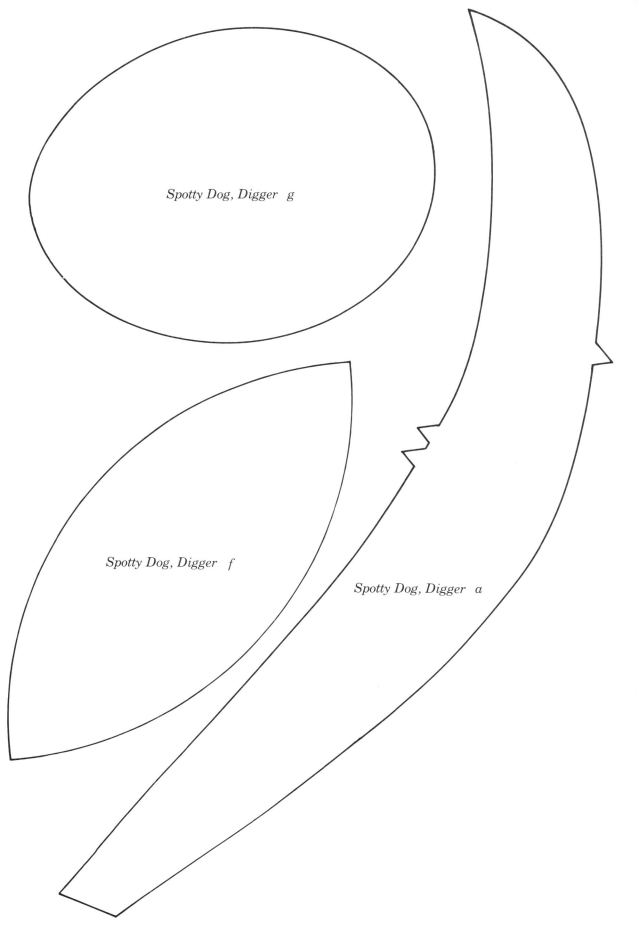

Spotty Dog, Digger g

Spotty Dog, Digger f

Spotty Dog, Digger a

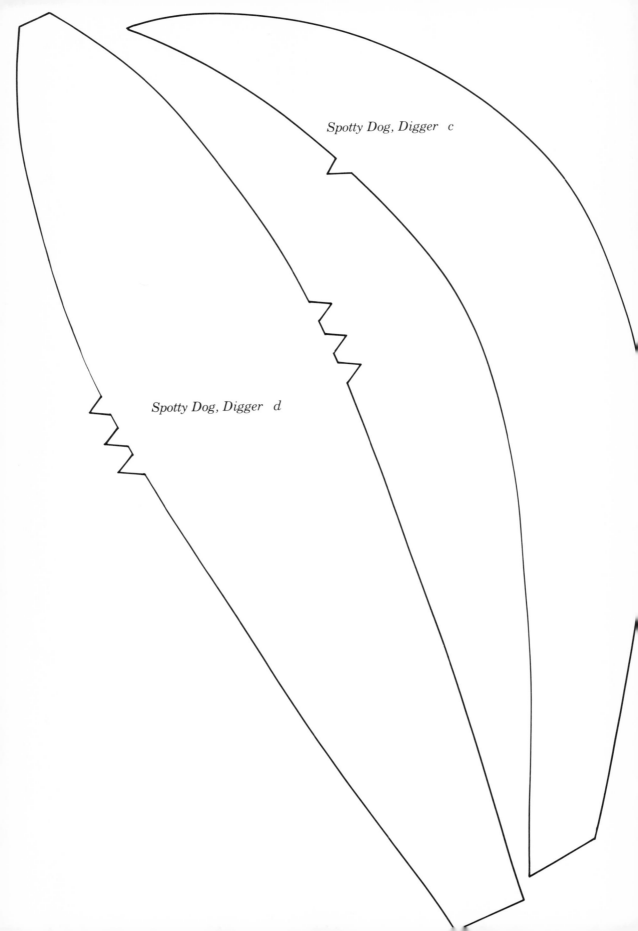

Spotty Dog, Digger c

Spotty Dog, Digger d

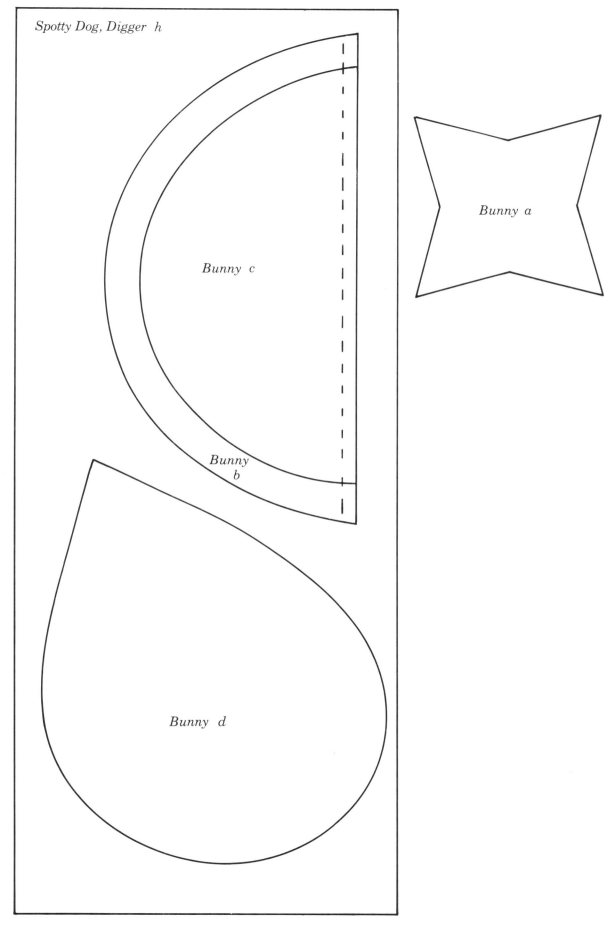

Spotty Dog, Digger h

Bunny c

Bunny b

Bunny d

Bunny a

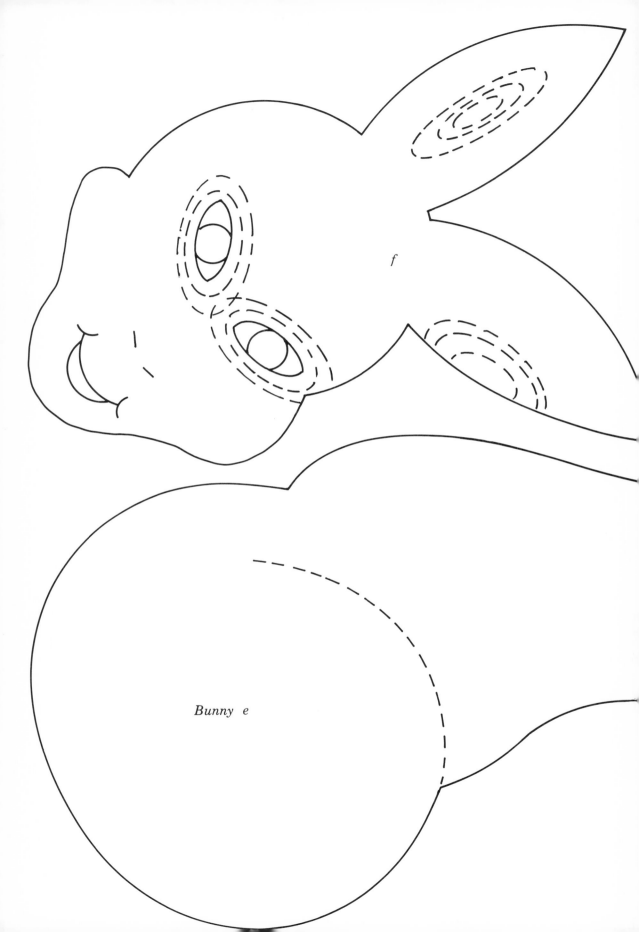

f

Bunny e

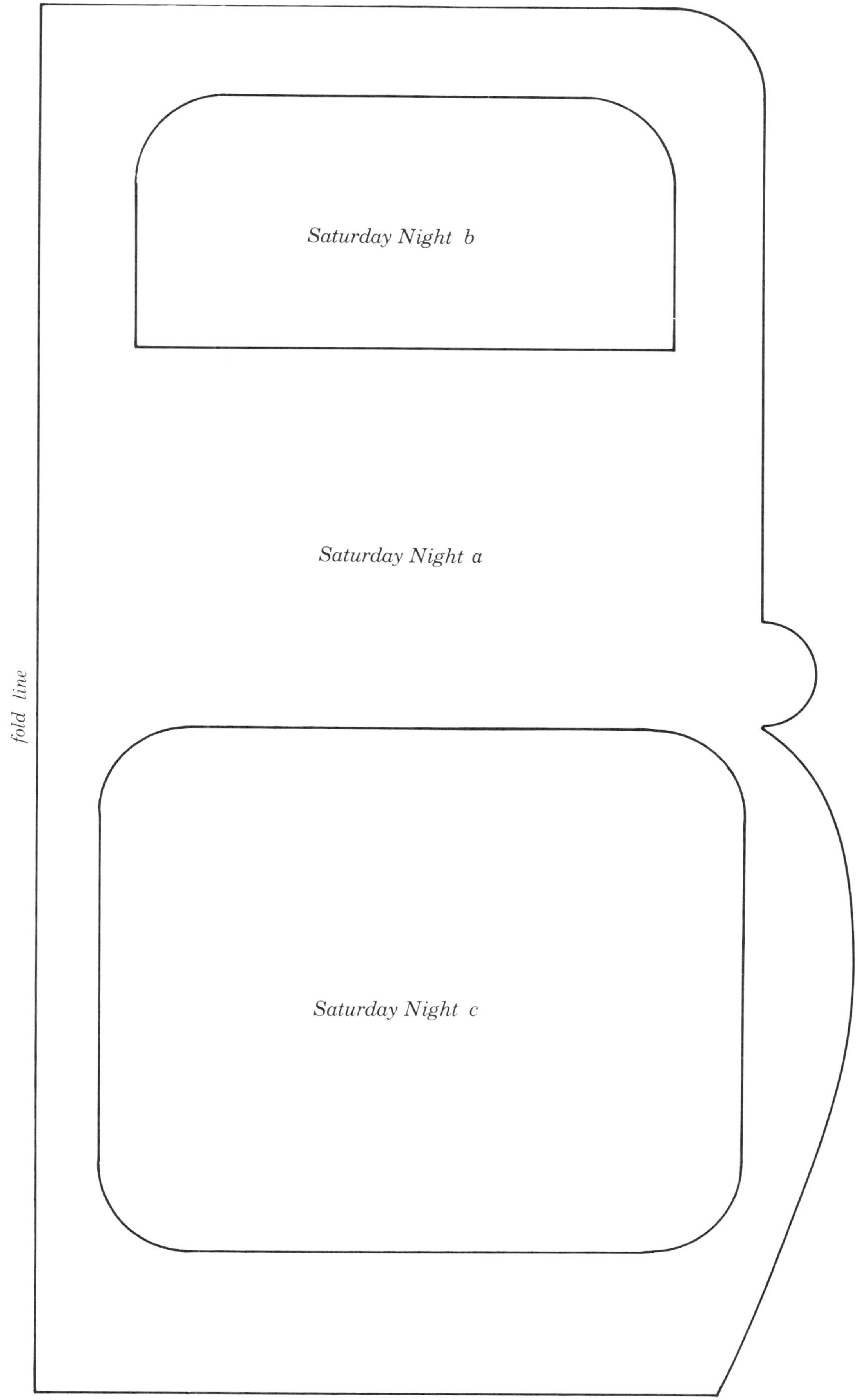

fold line

Saturday Night b

Saturday Night a

Saturday Night c

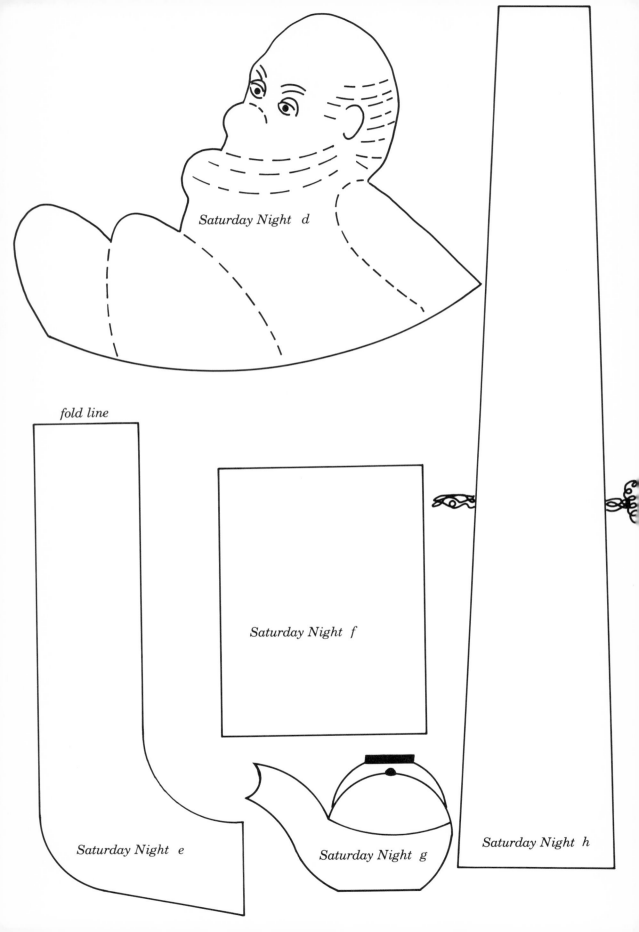

Saturday Night d

fold line

Saturday Night f

Saturday Night e

Saturday Night g

Saturday Night h

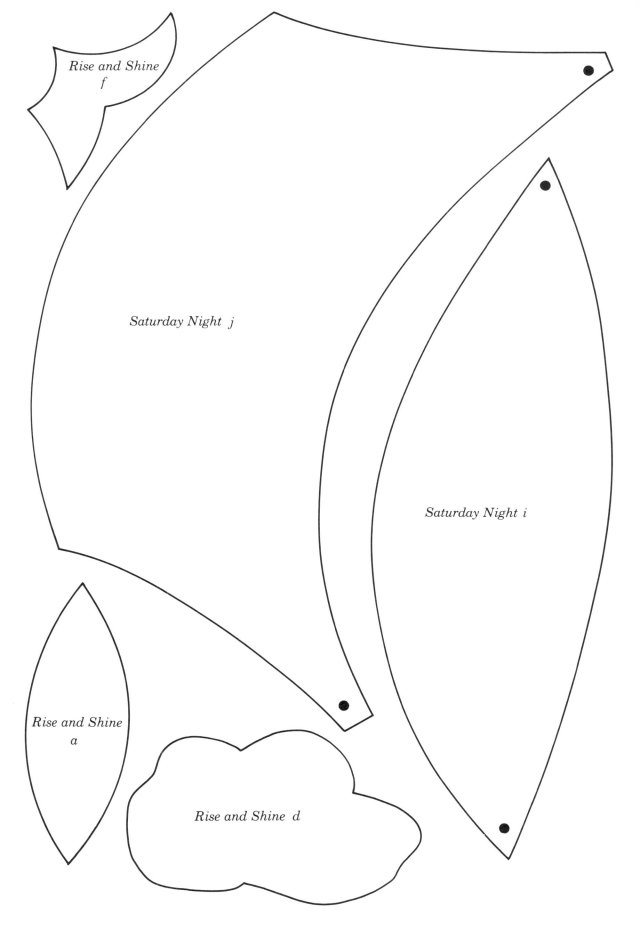

Rise and Shine
f

Saturday Night j

Saturday Night i

Rise and Shine
a

Rise and Shine d

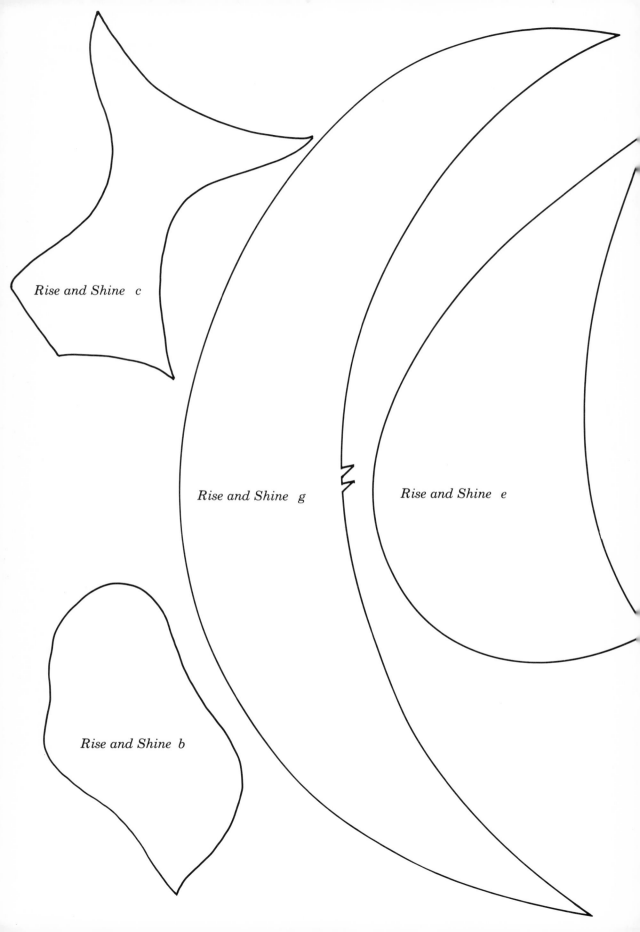

Rise and Shine c

Rise and Shine g

Rise and Shine e

Rise and Shine b

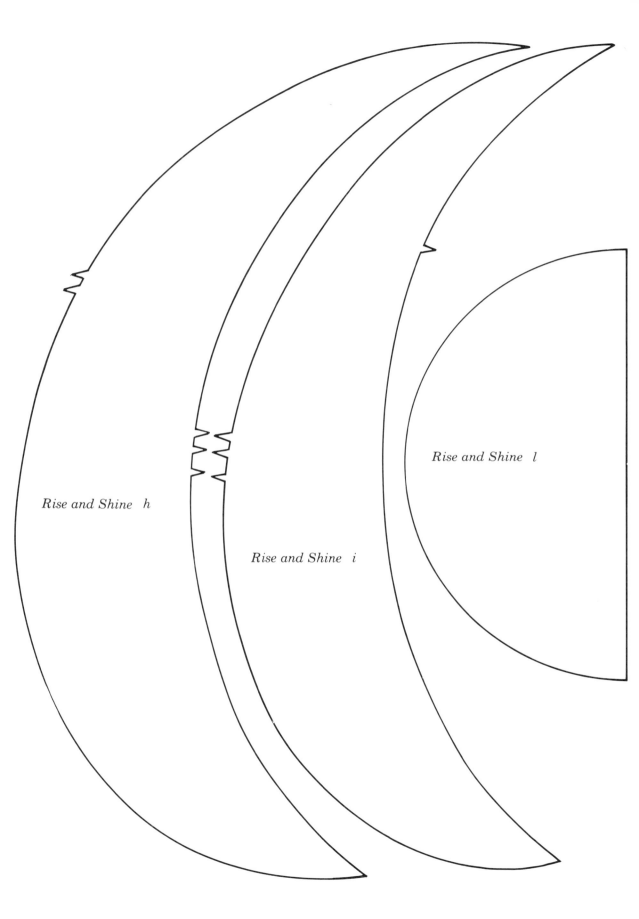

Rise and Shine   h

Rise and Shine   i

Rise and Shine   l

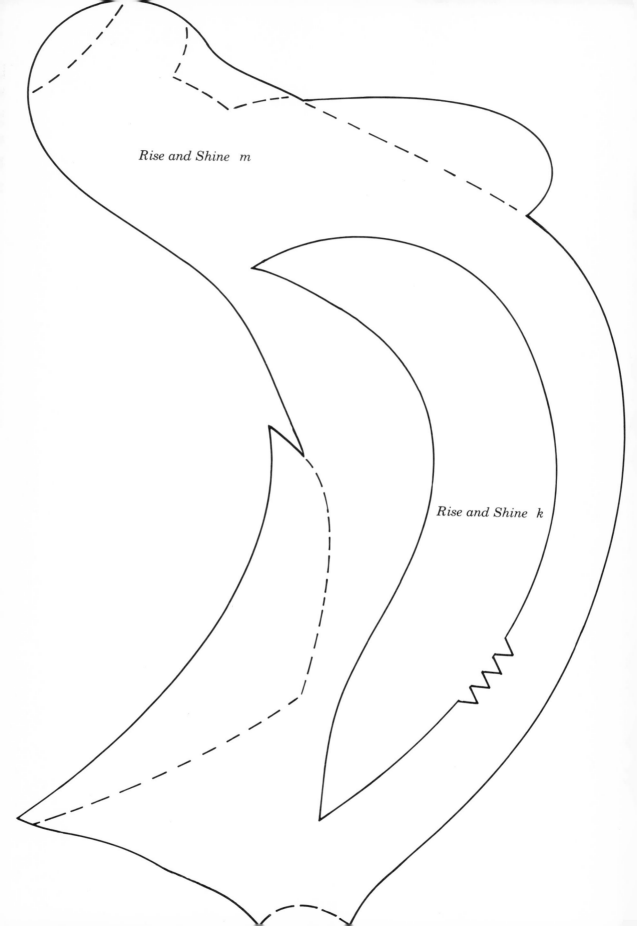

Rise and Shine   m

Rise and Shine   k

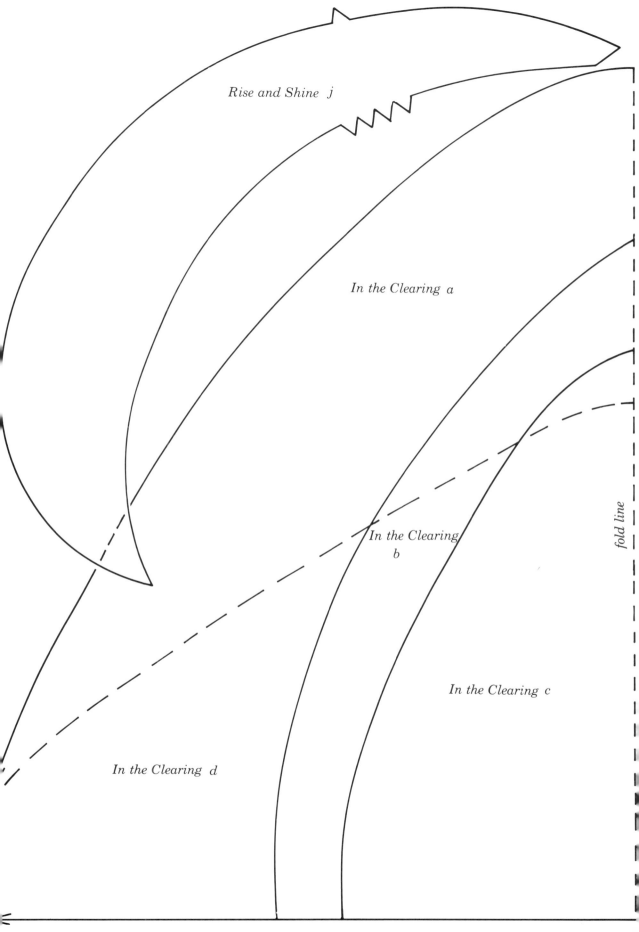

Rise and Shine *j*

In the Clearing *a*

In the Clearing *b*

In the Clearing *c*

In the Clearing *d*

fold line

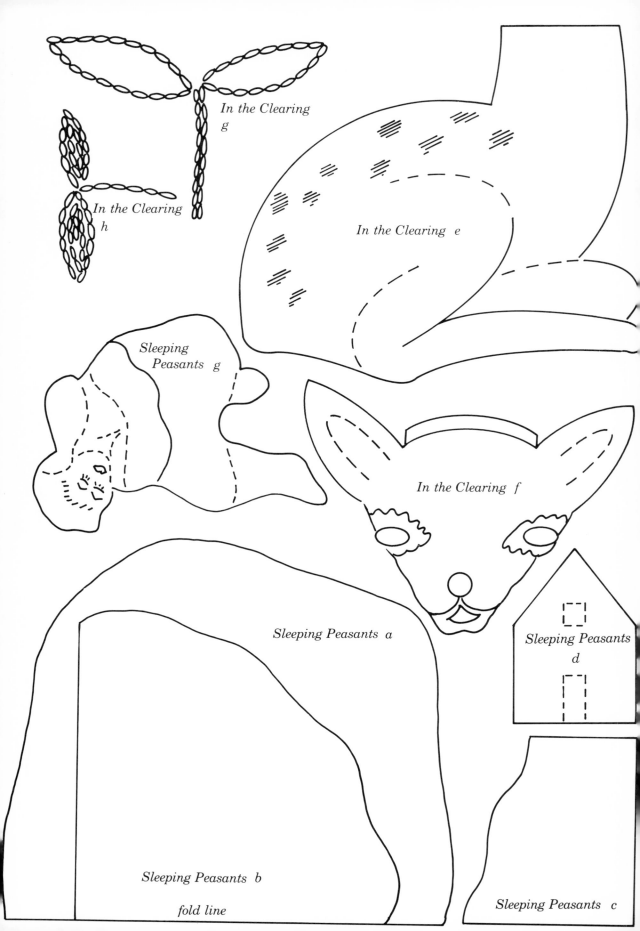

In the Clearing
g

In the Clearing
h

In the Clearing e

Sleeping
Peasants g

In the Clearing f

Sleeping Peasants a

Sleeping Peasants
d

Sleeping Peasants b

fold line

Sleeping Peasants c

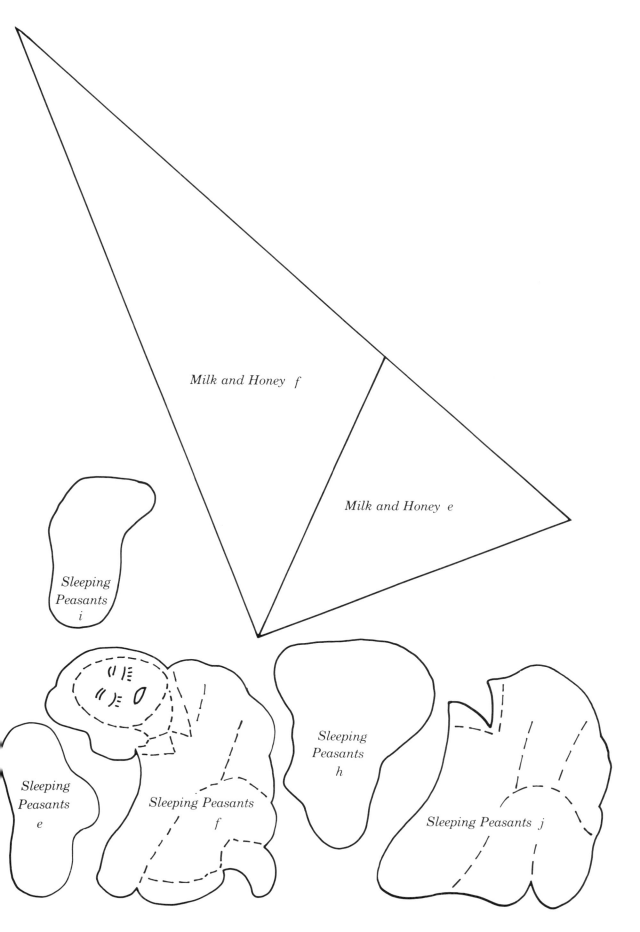

Milk and Honey f

Milk and Honey e

Sleeping
Peasants
i

Sleeping
Peasants
e

Sleeping Peasants
f

Sleeping
Peasants
h

Sleeping Peasants j

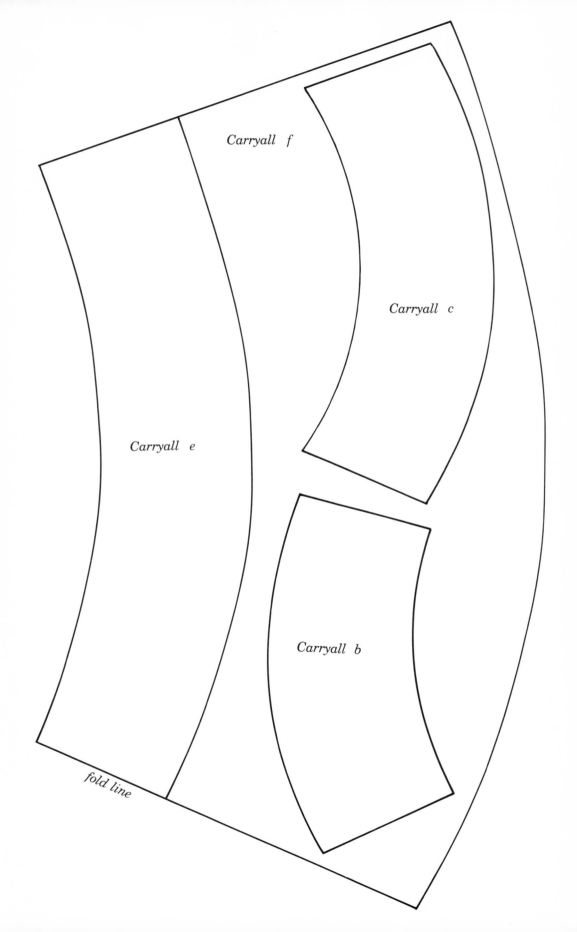

Carryall f

Carryall c

Carryall e

Carryall b

fold line

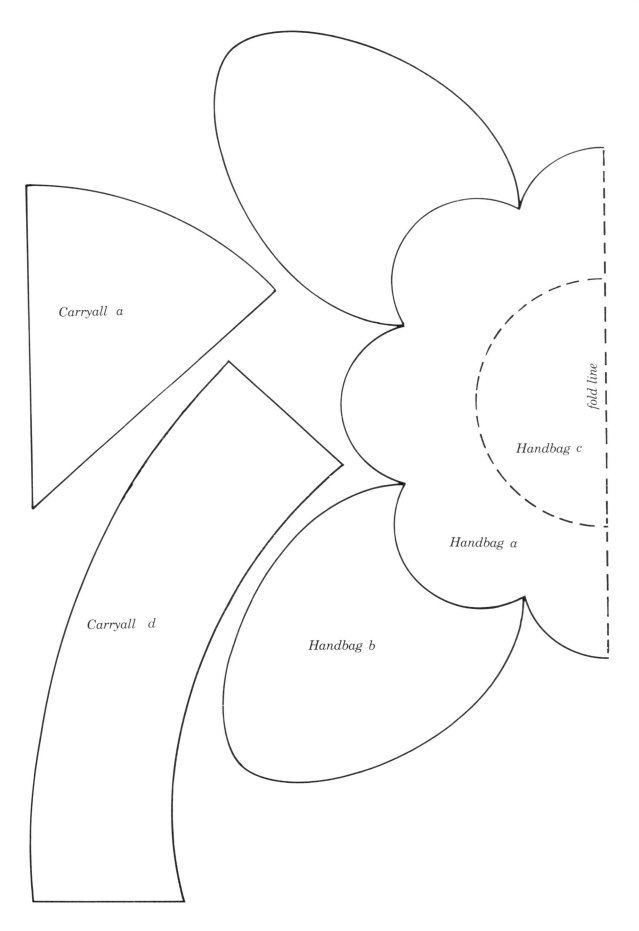

Carryall a

Carryall d

Handbag b

Handbag a

Handbag c

fold line

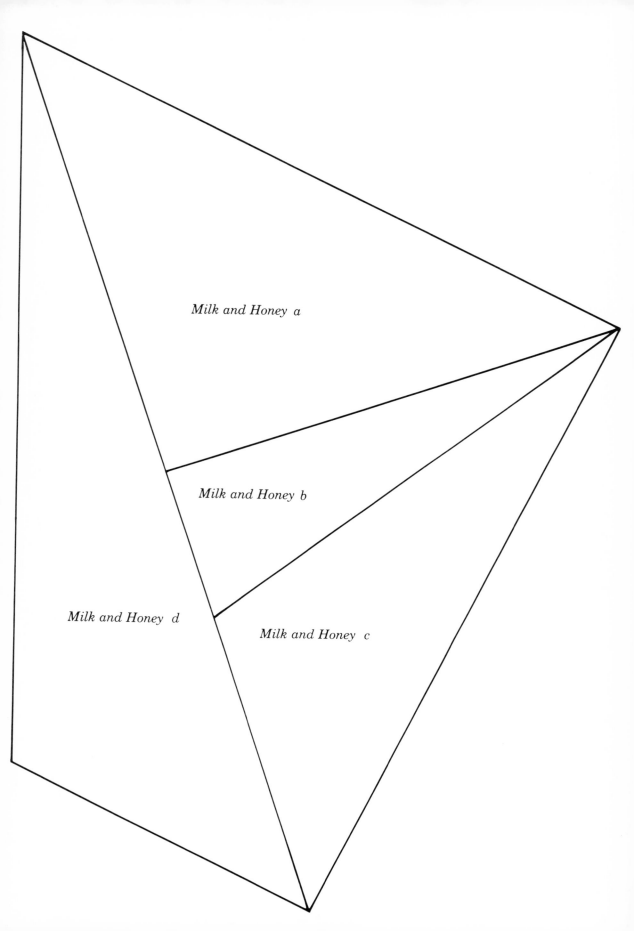

Milk and Honey a

Milk and Honey b

Milk and Honey d

Milk and Honey c

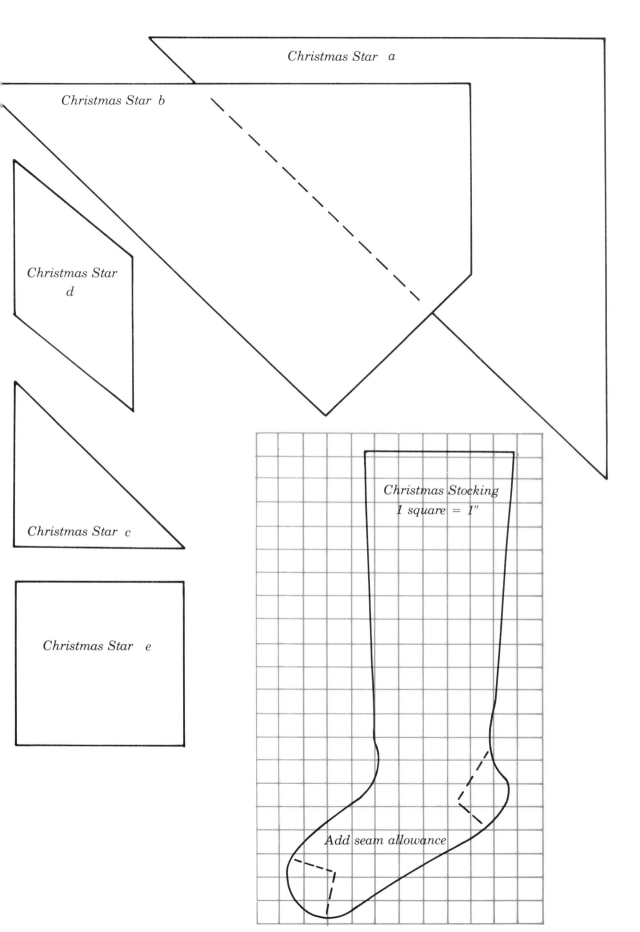

Christmas Star a

Christmas Star b

Christmas Star
d

Christmas Star c

Christmas Star e

Christmas Stocking
1 square = 1"

Add seam allowance

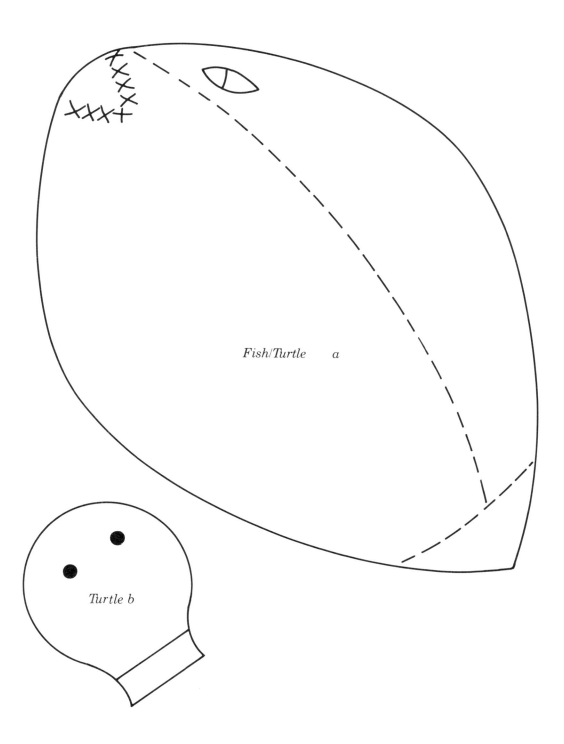

Fish/Turtle   *a*

Turtle b

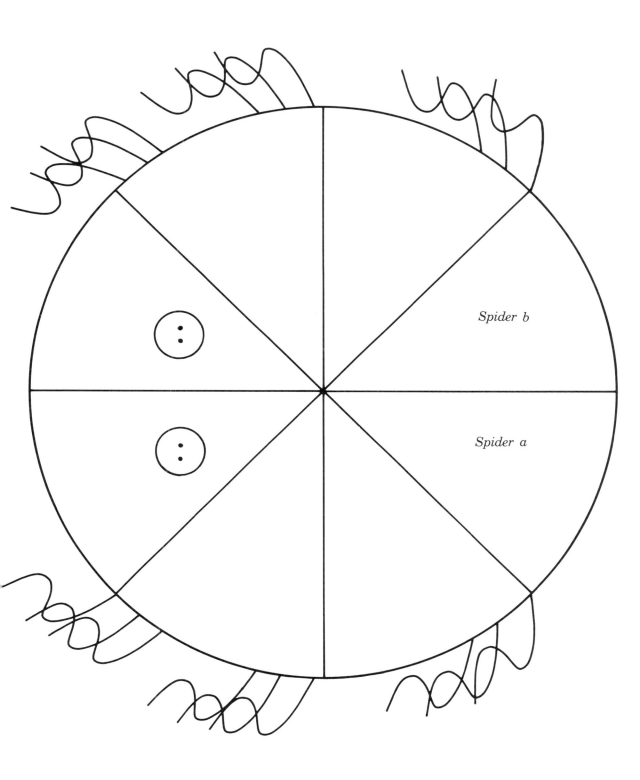